D1831778

Human Nature and Human Development: A Philosophical Quest

Human Nature and Human Development: A Philosophical Quest

Maithreyi Krishnaraj

KALPAZ

©**Author**
All rights reserved. No part of this work may be reproduced, stored, adapted, or transmitted in any form or by any means, electronic, mechanical, photocopying, micro-filming recording or otherwise, or translated in any language, without the prior written permission of the copyright owner and the publisher. The book is sold subject to the condition that it shall not, by way of trade or otherwise, be lent, resold, hired out, or otherwise circulated without the prior publisher's written consent in any form of binding or cover other than that in which it is published.

The views and opinions expressed in this book are author(s) own and the facts reported by them have been verified to the extent possible, and the publishers are not in any way liable for the same.

ISBN: 978-93-5128-222-8

Price: ₹ 720

First Published, 2017

Published by

Kalpaz Publications
C-30, Satyawati Nagar,
Delhi – 110052
E-mail: kalpaz@hotmail.com
Ph.: 9212142040

Printed at: G. Print Process, Delhi

Cataloging in Publication Data—DK
Courtesy: D.K. Agencies (P) Ltd. <docinfo@dkagencies.com>

Krishna Raj, Maithreyi., author.
Human nature and human development : a philosophical quest / Maithreyi Krishnaraj.
pages cm
Includes bibliographical references.
ISBN 9789351282228

1. Psychology—Religious aspects—Buddhism. 2. Buddhist philosophy. I. Title.

BQ4570.P76K75 2016 DDC 294.33615 23

Contents

Human Nature and Human Development: A Philosophical Quest

(Ancient wisdom and its contemporary relevance)[1]

Maithreyi Krishnaraj

I have traversed a difficult, terrain, trying to interpret who we are, what we are and why we are here. Ultimately, it is up to us to choose what we regard as most useful for us to save ourselves and save the world we live in. The essay concludes by realising that we sink or sail together with all other beings and non-beings. The Sun that gives us life will one day become a cold star but until then let us not raid this Earth. May be tomorrow armed with the new knowledge that science gives us and coupled with the wisdom of the ages, we open a window to the universe and bow in all humility to the grand enactment of which we in this 'pale blue dot' are a part.

Voyager 1 on Feb 14, 1990 left our planetary neighbourhood for the fringes of the solar system. Engineers turned it around for a last look at its home planet. Voyager 1 was about 6.4 billion kilometers away and approximately 32 degrees above the ecliptic plane when it captured the portrait of our world. Earth appeared as a tiny point of light –a crescent only 0.12 pixels in size. Carl Sagan's portal in You Tube narrates a lyrical account of our earth and human life.

1. Dedicated to the Dalai Lama whose life and works have inspired me on my own life's journey. I first came across "Light of Asia" by Edwin Arnold, presented to me by my father when I was nine years old and since then Buddhist philosophy as part of the Indian tradition has left a deep impact on me.

Acknowledgements

I thank my niece Geeta Tupil from Canada who helped me source some useful references and details of texts of some authors not available here.

To Channamma providing details for one or two missing references, I express my gratitude.

Objectives of this Work

The essay attempts to re-examine our current notions of human development and human nature and our position in the world. Human development is a broader, more inclusive concept than the discredited economic growth as a measure of a society's development but it is nevertheless limited in scope as it does not foreground the ethical basis of development.

This ethical basis we argue here is the understanding, valuing and conforming to the essential inter-connectedness of all living and non-living matter. It follows then that one's well being and fulfillment as a human being is 'dependent' on the welfare of other living and non-living matter. This interconnectedness is illustrated by drawing on the Buddhist concept of 'dependent origination' that is, nothing exists by itself. This is further elaborated through the related concept of 'sunyata': that nothing has an intrinsic identity by itself, standing alone as it were. To follow the ethic of altruism is to build bridges with each other. The essay also draws on biology, psychology and evolutionary psychology and philosophy to understand first, the nature of the human being and the human's relatedness to all others and thereby place where we are in the order of things. Writings on ecology and environment further expose our assumption that we are somehow above nature as an ego centric view.

According to evolutionary psychology, human beings have developed a brain that is extremely adaptable to circumstances. The adaptation comes in the form of a reciprocal altruism–a tendency inherent within us, though the precise contents of it are not hard wired in us. Ethics addresses our dilemma of how we should conduct ourselves. Buddhist cannons emphasise 'right living' to promote harmony and greater social progress. Translated into our approach to human development, this essay argues for an understanding of our inherent relatedness in order to value not just ourselves as independent beings but as part of a vast network in the cosmos. A corollary is that we cannot sustain a viable, stable, dynamic society unless we also grant that every person has 'human rights' and the right to flourish and by implication we cannot really develop our full potential unless we reduce inequality based on social structure where opportunities are not available to everyone. This is the basic ethic the essay tries to stress drawing from different philosophical cogitations. Among these, Buddha was foremost in advocating egalitarianism.

The implication is that the true development of the human being and human society has to take on board the welfare of others. A development model that ignores this fundamental premise is non-development. Freedom and opportunity has to be available to all. Social conflicts arise because of inequalities and inequities. One's development depends not just on what one individual possesses or what one receives to enhance or add to one's starting point. Current work on ecology and environment has demonstrated this truth that we owe our existence to the well-being of all that surrounds us. If out of our greed or what we think as our necessity, we raid this gift, we end up poorer. The essay tries to look at the concept of human development from many perspectives available in science, psychology, philosophy and evolution. Buddhist ethics and Buddhist philosophy emphasise our moral responsibility in the basic doctrines of 'mahayana' strand of Buddhism which survived in India for several centuries. Likewise our Upanishads emphasise our connection to the universal consciousness. Against this, the logical fallacy of mainstream economics view of growth stands exposed for its notion of the individual as a stand alone entity, arriving as it were in society as an independent, self sufficient actor. The teacher learns from the student; the child learns from the parent; the parent learns from the child; plants and animals nourish us. Rivers, mountains, forests safeguard our planet. If we ignore their interests out of a human centric valuation, we are ascribing to ourselves a right of overlordship over others. If we share a kinship with non-human things then we must also apply the same to all human beings and abjure discrimination against some. Human welfare should be available to all.

Chapter - 1

Introduction

We are familiar with critiques of development that focuses only on economic growth. Growth, conventionally measured by GDP primarily includes the material output or as Leo Huberman (1936) put it “man’s worldly goods”. The shift towards human development as the measure of development was a big step forward but it still has within it economic criteria but modified to include non-monetary components such as education and health, to the earlier per capita income as the basic components of human development. To this was added later ‘participation’ and some indices on participation in political life were added. The process of creating worldly goods, who in effect contributes most and at what cost, what precisely is the composition of that output and who gets compensated for what, are questions that arise when we draw the curtain open to look at the process. In other words we are saying it is not a mere question of the end result of a particular type of growth of the economy and then acting to redistribute the product more equitably to different sections of the society. It is often postulated for instance that inequality does not matter so long as there is a minimum obtainable for all or as it used to be put everyone has ‘basic needs’ satisfied. If by human development we mean on the other hand, the development of human potential we are hard put to define what really this potential is. Such a potential can only be gauged when given a chance to manifest itself.

Economics as a discipline has some basic premises: it takes the individual as the unit of behaviour and assumes this individual to stand alone, free standing as it were without the history of all that went into making that individual. Individual choice governed by rationality, as determining economic action then obscures the forces of social, cultural, settings within which individuals actually act. Maximising the returns in any activity is the goal of rational economic behaviour. In reality, households, poor groups and women exert to maximise not returns but well being of the group to which they consider themselves as accountable. Looked at conventionally through economic calculus they are not 'efficient' but viewed as actions geared towards survival in an in-hospitable environment, they in fact uphold the economy and make possible the more visible so called efficient sectors.

We are used to the dual sectors–the one more advanced and the other less advanced in terms of technology and productivity but why does the economy create two sectors?

Every individual participating in economic activities (whether recognised as such) if defined as aiding survival of the human beings in that unit, they are part of 'development' activities–the underside that upholds the other surface sides. In other words, development, if in its process intensifies the human cost of survival for a large section of society, is mal-development. This situation may be remedied by anti-poverty programmes or through enhancing social indicators for the deprived or by other palliatives. However, these will do nothing to alter the basic premises of that development model.

How does one then redefine a good development model? 'Work' is intrinsically an important aspect of being human. The Bhagwat Gita emphasises this in extolling karma yoga. Our task is to do what we can and leave the results to manifest themselves. In other words, to do the right thing *without being motivated solely by results sought.* It does not mean we do not care for the outcome. Human development would then imply how that work is conducted in a way that enhances one's well being. For example, a corporate executive may work like 'mad' for five days then take two days off to relax. What human development would say as philosophers have maintained, is that those five days of work should be rewarding in terms of its ability to help one survive, move ahead, be able to use one's opportunities, to develop one's capabilities and functioning with enough scope for freedom to have alternate choices; such work should also be not be demeaning, should not involve exploitative human relations and where the power relations induced by unequal wealth and political power should not find scope for play. Under-development is not just lack of capabilities but the lack of opportunity to even engage in building capability. These raise issues of what we mean by skill, who defines skill, who defines which skill is to be rewarded. Selling soaps as a management executive in a market economy, fetches more rewards than that of a mother diligently nurturing children to make them capable of participating as worker and as citizen.

Human development by this perspective is not the end product of a course of 'development' but is part and parcel of that process; the ends and means are not separable.

Let us now explore a little about how different disciplines understand our place in the world–where we came from and what our special features are. Given these different perspectives we have to see how to make the best use of our heritage from various sources.

Chapter - 2

We as 'Humans' are Part of the Biological System

We are biological beings sharing life with other living systems. A living being unfolds a magnificent design. The craftsman who assembled species, was natural selection, acting upon mutations and re-combinations of genes, through vast number of steps over long periods of time. The genetic heritage of LIFE is a living library. The sheer number of genes prescribing a tree or a human being runs into tens of thousands. The nucleotide pairs composing them are, the genetic code for the life giving enzymes. These vary among species from one billion to ten billion. If the DNA helices in one cell of say a creature like a mouse were placed end on end and enlarged to the size of a wrapping string, they would extend to nine hundred kilometers. Measured in terms of sheer information, the genome of a cell is comparable to all editions of Encyclopaedia Britannica since its inception in 1768!

There is a genetic unity of life. All organisms have descended from the same distant ancestor, similar to single cell microbe. All species share certain fundamental molecular traits. Their tissue is divided into cells, whose enveloping lipid membranes regulate exchange with the outside environment. The molecular machinery that generates energy is similar. Because all organisms have descended from a common ancestor, it is correct to say that when the biosphere began to think, humanity was born. Our place in nature viewed from an ethical perspective is to value creation and safeguard it. (Wilson, 2003)

At the same time, it is diversity of life that is the key to the maintenance of the world as we know it. It took a billion years to evolve. It is diversity of life that builds and saturates the rain forest, carries life beyond to the harshest environments. The deep unlighted caves around the world, harbour untold insects; the harshest deserts of the world are home to unique ensemble of insects, lizards and flowering plants. Arch bacteria occupy the boiling water of mineral hot springs and volcanic vents in the deep sea. Life adapts its self to such immensely varied environments. Each kind of plant and animal is linked in the food web to only a small part of other species. Eliminate one species and another species increases in number to take its place. However, in an eroding eco-system, the restorative power of fauna and flora break down because their capacity to reinvigorate a degenerate system depends on the existence of enough number of species. Had there been no human interference the background extinction is one species per one million species. Human activity has increased extinction between 1000 to 10,000 times and the number of doomed species per year is 27,000. (Wilson, 1992). As of 2012, it was predicted that 25 per cent of all mammalian species would be extinct in twenty years. We overlook the services that eco-systems provide us. This life sustaining matrix is built of green plants, and legions of micro organisms. Wilson's commentary 'Social Conquest of the Earth' (2013) and 'The Meaning of Human Existence' (2014) sounded alerts on the destructive effects of our ways of life. From 1950-2011, world population increased from 2.5 billion to 7 billion and by the end of twenty-first century might reach 9 billion. This massive growth of human population has had more impact on bio-diversity than any other single factor.

The typical human is home to a vast array of microbes. If we count them we will find that microbial cells outnumber our own by a factor of 10. In that sense we are only 10 per cent human and the rest of us is made up of microbes. We do not realise this because micro-organisms are extremely small. Though they make up 90 per cent of our cells, they are not 90 per cent of our bulk. (Judson, 2009)

Micro organisms enrich the soil and create the very air we breathe. We need therefore an environment ethic. Humanity evolved within living communities and our body functions are adjusted to the environment already created. We need therefore an environment ethic. What biologists tell us are: (1) as species, we are all connected to each other, and (2) there is immense diversity of life and this diversity needs to be protected because if species diminish our own fate is in jeopardy.

In the eloquent words of Wilson:

"What is morality but the command of conscience seasoned by a rational examination of consequences? What is a fundamental precept but one that serves all generations - an enduring environmental ethic that aims to preserve not only the health and freedom of our species but access to the world in which the human spirit was born?" (p. 29, Wilson, 1992). Wilson argued "...the ethic from which moral decisions spring, is a norm or standard of behaviour in support of a value and value in turn depends on purpose. The purpose whether personal or global, whether urged by conscience or graven in sacred script, expresses the image we hold of ourselves and our place in society. (Wilson, 2003)

There is an indeterminacy and both continuity and discontinuity with culture and biology. Where does biology end and where does culture begin is difficult to assess. Some hold that as human beings we all have the same fundamental drives: drive to acquire, drive to bond, drive to comprehend and make sense of the world and drive to defend. (Nohria and Lawrence, 2001).

Recent work in the philosophy of biology underscores the brilliant way in which our bodies orchestrate in ways to make organisms work in co-ordination, even while each organ has a specific function. The volume "Life and Organicism" (2009) explored the philosophical foundations of biological thinking.

Chapter - 3

Evolutionary Psychology

The new Darwinian synthesis tries to explore how the human being has a built in moral core. (Wright, 1994). Evolutionary psychology is like quantum physics in molecular biology, a body of scientific theory and fact, but unlike them it is also a way of seeing everyday life. What are really the questions that plague us?

1. Are men and women really built for monogamy?
2. What is the explanatory logic behind office politics?
3. Why did natural selection give us that vast guilt repository known as conscience? Is it truly a guide to moral behaviour?
4. Is hierarchy inherent in human society?
5. What are the different inclinations of men and women in areas such as friendship and ambition?
6. Why do we exclude such large groups of people?
7. Deception, self-deception and the unconscious mind, various psychopathologies such as depression, neurotic behaviour and becoming paranoid- are these natural?

Evolutionary psychologists discern a deeper unity within the different species. Anthropologists have noted recurring themes in culture: a thirst for approval, a capacity for guilt. We may call these and other such universals 'The knobs of human nature'. How do figure out how these knobs work? How do they get set? Genetic differences do exist but the larger role is exerted by genetic commonalities. We do have a generic, species wide development programme that absorbs information from their social environment and adjusts the maturing mind accordingly. Oddly the future progress in grasping the importance of environment will come from thinking about genes.

Human nature comes in two forms both of which have a tendency to get ignored:

1. There is the kind that is so pervasively apparent as to be taken for granted (guilt for example).
2. There is the kind whose very function is to generate differences among people as they grow up.

Human nature consists of knobs and mechanisms for turning the knobs and both are invisible in their own way. There is a reason why human nature has been slow to come to light: the basic evolutionary logic common to people everywhere is opaque to introspection. Natural selection appears to have hidden our true selves from our conscious selves. (Wright, 1994, p. 9)

Edward Wilson (2004) refers to two conceptions of human nature that were part of western thought. Theologians had a pessimistic view of human nature as dark angels in animal bodies that needed redemption to gain immortality. To them human beings are a mix of good and evil propensities which we have to sort out. On the other hand intellectuals doubted whether some thing we can dub as 'human nature' exists at all. To them our brain is a blank state, driven by a few elementary passions but otherwise acts like a computer, to create the mind. We learn from individual experience and culture. Most people believed that what we are is the result of our cumulative learned response to environment and historical contingency. An alternative naturalistic view gained prominence which saw the brain as a blank slate, entirely biological, structured through evolution by natural selection. Human nature is composed of the complex biases of passion plus learning propensities, loosely referred to as 'instincts' created over millions of years right from the time human beings were hunter gatherers. Hence, they bear the archaic imprint of the biological heritage of our species. Human nature can be understood through the use of the scientific method. A discipline known as socio-biology holds that culture evolves in response to both environment and history but at the same time guided by inborn biases of being a human being. This approach of evolutionary psychology came to be known a socio-biology.

The issues socio-biology dealt with were

What are human instincts? How do they align to create human nature? Till the 1970's these questions were not taken up. The development of neuro-science coupled with evolutionary biology tried to explain why the brain works in the odd ways it does and not in some other way. The puzzle of human nature can be resolved only if scientific explanations embrace both the *how* of neuro-science and the *why* of evolutionary biology. We have to figure out in what precise manner these tendencies in mental development have shaped culture. The way human beings lived in bands, learnt to use fire, invented tools, perfected language, reached all the continents betray the concurrence of genes plus culture.

Wilson's own pioneering work with ants led him to marvel at the complexity and precision of instincts in shaping insect lives. His conclusion was that societies are populations governed by a combination of generics and ecology. There is no doubt there is a vast difference between insects and vertebrates with respect to their systems of communication, that leads one to believe that socio-biology can be derived from population and behavioural psychology. We can then see the contrast between animal behaviour and the behaviour of human beings. It expounds the biological basis of behaviour. Wilson did not approve of eugenics or social Darwinism that emerged from political and religious ideology.

Phillip Rieff (2009) maintained that Charles Horton Cooley's work establishes the connection between human nature and the social order and this is really a reflection on how the imagination of human beings helps towards constant adjustment of social responses. We have two channels - heredity and what we get from society. Our mode of life does not alter the heredity of our children. Is the interaction and heredity antagonistic? One important feature among humans is the long infancy which gives time for teachability. Instinct is expressed as emotion. Human conduct cannot be explained entirely on the basis of instincts. We organise instinct through reason. In that sense our instincts are plastic.

Cooley in 1902 published his classic "Human Nature and the Social Order". It was subsequently revised in 1922. He argued that

that there is a flash point at which human imagination ignites to produce the infinitely adjustable social temperature. That flash point can account for the horrors of concentration camp or the warmth of the family. Cooley does not presume an ontology but talks of social order itself. He contended that there is no basis for assuming a human nature superior to social order. As a sociologist, unlike the philosophers, psychologists, theologians and holy men, examined the dynamics which make this mode of self understanding socially necessary. Thus, primarily by linking doctrines of human nature to social order, he asserted that both were widely diffused. Every social order produces a doctrine of human nature, an imagery of individual development implicit in that order. There are combinations and complexities of fix and drift that we should treat historically and empirically. Doctrines of human nature in all varieties can be known only at the expense of belief. They are embarrassing expedients, which every social order creates until our own, to give shape and colour to the emptiness that might shake our ego through uncertainty. Every culture produces an insulation of experience. This is often better expressed through Art. In Buddhist doctrine, the panic and emptiness can be experienced to become integral part of the religious task from childhood.

Mastery is taught in a variety of ways through appropriate pedagogy beginning with parental training. In the history of American social-science, the study of children became important because of insights it gave into development of social communication.[1] Thus, the naked ego is clothed and protected from ontological emptiness. The social order clothes the actors born into it in the self understanding that makes them reluctant to shed it even for the rare privilege of a glimpse into nothingness. Cooley maintained that every society, produces out of its own structure the myth within which it is empowered to live. This is possible because self feeling is fused with enough social strength to keep the individual in civility and self respect and thus ensure social peace. It is the control of hostility by allegiance to a rule based order. It is a kind of mass manufacture of the emperor's clothes. The emperor in the story was made to believe by a wily tailor that his nakedness was actually clothed till a child declared that he was naked. There is nothing to believe except the utility of belief itself. Just as the Jesuits spread education to keep the church's authority, Cooley holds that contemporary psychiatrists propagate the idea of two natures within us- the undiluted nature and the refined nature after treatment. Thus Cooley's contention is that our ideas of human nature are the products used for polemical institutional uses. Gestures do not have their primary function of expressing emotion; they are now part of complex tools of social communication. The body is not a 'self' in itself; it becomes so only in relation to others. This is what Buddhists say, "I am what I am because of what you are." To sum up Cooley's ideas: society in its immediate aspects is a relation among personal ideas. Society exists in my mind as the contact and reciprocal influence of certain ideas named "I". It exists in your mind as a similar group and so in every mind. In other words the imagination that people have of one another are the solid facts of society. It is the result of three aspects of consciousness: (i) self consciousness: what I think of myself, (ii) social consciousness: what I think of others, and (iii) public consciousness: a collective view organised in a communicating group. Cooley's doctrine of society is an affair of consciousness, it is necessarily ideas about himself which he or she attributes to others. The idea of self has two principal elements– the imagination of our appearance to others, the imagination of the judgement of that appearance, for example, some sort of self feeling such as pride or mortification. Public consciousness is the result of communication and discussion which reside in the common idea of persons in their organisation. Ideas have definition and reality only in their relationship to other ideas. Values that attach to any idea can only be defined in terms of values that belong to the whole structure to which the idea belongs. The self is not an immediate character of the mind but arises through the imagination of the ideas which others entertain of the individual. Without communication the mind does not develop into a human nature. Social ideas and their organisation are not presentations of a reality lying outside but the solid facts of society. One is not first an individual and then social. The mind itself arises only through the social interaction. Cooley found in consciousness, a social process within which self and others arise. Regarding the self as the ideas others entertain about the self and of the self on others, the self becomes simply the ideas of each upon others within the mind. It is the social process of growth and integration. The question still remains: do the self and others lie within the mind or mind itself as a psychical phase of experience is an outgrowth of primitive human communication.

Darwin's theory of natural selection can be summed up in his own words as 'Multiply, vary, let the strongest live and weakest die'. Your entire body is much more complexly harmonious than any product of human design created by hundreds of thousands of incremental advances and each increment was an accident; each tiny step between your ancestral bacterium and you, just happened to help some intermediate ancestral bacterium more profusely to get its genes into the next generation. Every organ inside you is tantamount to art- your heart, lungs, your stomach etc. Various mental organs constitute the human mind. As an organ it inclines people to love their offspring. This is species typical and this gives human kind their psychic unity.

The overriding criterion of organic design is fitness. A feature that is adaptive today, may not be adaptive tomorrow. And all along the way the definition of good design remains the same. There are thousands and thousands of genes that build the brain and govern neurotransmitters and other hormones- they define our mental organs and are here for a reason. And, the reason is they goaded our ancestors in getting their genes into the next generation. The basic way we feel about each other, the basic kind of things we think about each other and say to each other are with us today by virtue of their positive contribution to genetic fitness. At some point extensive male parental investment entered our evolutionary heritage, not as high as that of the female but more than that of the average primate.

Characteristically, natural selection has a cost-benefit calculus, transmitted into a sensation of love, not just for the child but also between man and woman. A huge majority–980 out of 1154 societies past and present have permitted a man to have more than one wife. Hence, 43 per cent of the population in 980 societies are polygamous cultures. So long as societies remain economically stratified, polygamy exists. The more egalitarian a society became, monogamy became the norm because all males have access to enough females to procreate. These are species typical, adaptations to maximise fitness but if we focus only on individual we cannot expect that person to maximise fitness. Natural selection cannot directly see an individual organism in a specific situation and cause behaviour to be adaptively tailored. It can give males a love of offspring. Adaptation is not fool proof. Natural selection can give women an attraction to muscle module or status module and the strength of these attractions depend on all kinds of germane factors. *"Human beings are not 'fitness' maximisers but adaptive executers"* (Wright, 1994, p. 107) Italics mine. The ever shifting but almost perennially uneven balance of affection and obligation between parent and child is one of life's deepest and most bitter sweet experiences.

If we argue that morality is grounded in biology why do moral codes differ so widely? This is because we have a deep sensitivity to social approval. The reason codes vary between cultures is they judge for historical reasons, different norms to be in the best interest of society or community. Who judges this? Here Wright ignores the role of social power and social institutions. Male dominance leads to female subordination in human societies. It is the feminist movement and feminist theorising that exposed this feature of human society to be not based on biology but social structure. Gender inequality (that is between men and women) has created a cost to society by the exploitation and oppression of women. It has denied women social and political power in ways that has not only prevented women's full development and potential, it has carried a cost to society by losing the full participation of women in society. Male dominance which feminist theorising terms "patriarchy" has held sway over much of human history, obscuring women's contribution and blocking their access to resources of nature and of society.

Feminist theorising about inequality between men and women opens another Pandora's box. It argues that inequality arises because of failure of society to value the enormous contribution by women in terms of care. The sexual division of labour confers unequal rewards and punishments to men and women which ignores real worth of women's contribution. Women bring forth future workers, through their labour of child birth and lactation, besides spending considerable energy in looking after children till they grow into adulthood. Krishnaraj (2001) tried to indicate how gender figures in economic theory and philosophy. Krishnaraj (2009) argued that the ethic of care is the basis of well-being of any society. It implies responsibility for oneself and others–a kind of balance between the two. Care, responsibility and compassion have to be part of citizenship values which women claim to have more of and masculine discourse dismisses as non-rational" (Krishnaraj, 2009).

Lewton (1991) declares that biology is really a form of ideology. In an earlier era the concept of 'race' was used to uphold the superiority of some and dismiss some as inferior in terms of natural endowment. Today the notion of race is held to be an invalid classification of humans. Blacks were treated as inferior until the time when Blacks struggled to obtain civil rights in the USA. The practice of Apartheid in South Africa which segregated Africans by white settlers had to be fought against. Anthropologists and demographers place the origin of the human being in its present form in Africa until migration to Europe bestowed white superiority on those who populated Europe. More than two-thirds of the world's population are after all black or brown.

The Role of Economic Theory

Economics as a discipline has been hugely concerned with 'development' whose goal was to reduce poverty through increasing the total production of society in question. This was not an unrealistic assumption. Poverty is a situation of vulnerability to those who undergo deprivation. The perennial debate about objectivity and subjectivity is barking up the wrong tree because the process of understanding reality is simultaneously both because both involve judgement and intuition. The notion that economics is objective arises because it deals with numbers and quantities which can be mathematically manipulated. There is merit in this approach as only through abstraction which eliminates complexity and isolates variables that interact, we get some degree of understanding the nature of the interaction. What distinguishes economics from other social disciplines is its methodology, namely putting out clearly its basic assumptions and the rules it applies. By and large the discipline has difficulty in making room for collective behaviour or altruistic behaviour. The greatest lacuna is the inability to incorporate gender concerns within economic development theory where it is still an externality. Present day notions of human capital approximates this but is confined to skill and knowledge and not female labour that produces new labour (Krishnaraj, 2001).

Why is macro economic theory blind?

Macro theory deals with aggregates and is blind to individuals, gender, sectors and location. Some of the reasons for economics are the following:

1. Perception of roles and their relative values influence allocations.
2. Perception of employers and workers influence wage determination.
3. Physical relocation of activities previously done outside market nexus exacerbate gender and childcare.
4. Economic theory till now did not deal with intra household allocations.
5. Economic theory deals mainly with production for the market and hence covers only a partial account of economic activity.
6. The opportunity cost of female labour is ignored. If women enter market production, this has consequences for childcare unless arrangements exist for childcare.
7. Efficiency of resource allocation in a free market economy is attempted through input levels that reflect the opportunity cost to society as a whole in reordering allocation. Most importantly economic theory ignores the institutional context-for example, bonded labour.
8. Additionally, economics is unable to deal with power satisfactorily because it is based on a certain notion of the individual as unconnected to social structure.
9. Another big lacunae is treating the environment as 'free' for us. Production for profit pushes the natural frontiers beyond bearable limits. Nature takes far longer than a generation or two to replace lost resources.
10. Other after effects of human interventions are climate change, ozone depletion, melting of glaziers- all of which disturb ecological balance.

A model of human development that commoditises natural resources is a dead end. The resources of our biosphere must be garnered rationally in full awareness of limits. Alas we have only lately realised these limits! (Krishnaraj, 2007) There is still time to learn from past mistakes. Recent advances in ecology and environment are discussed in detail later in this essay to establish our connections with nature.

Was it always this way?

Long before people signed formal contracts, friendship, affection, trust influenced human relations. Wright calls this reciprocal altruism. When we trace the connection between our genes to our brains we may be able to understand our behaviour better on how this knob turns. The question that arises is: why has natural selection given us a flexible conscience rather than fixing its contents innately? Why and how are the morality knobs of human nature tenable? Why has natural selection made morality malleable? Why did it not hard wire it in the brain?

Reality is more complicated. We know people cheat, lie, steal and prosper. The pay offs depend on the social environment. We would expect natural selection to favour developmental plasticity of the traits regulating altruistic and cheating tendencies and responses to these tendencies. A society where everyone without exception cheats is a logical impossibility. Whatever the reason, natural selection endowed our species with flexible, reciprocally altruistic strategies. It is flexibility that raises their value. Victorian morality was possible in a steady, small society. In the present context of urban and more fluid settlements, it is different. In a highly moral society, daily life involves many acts of courtesy and altruism because meanness and dishonesty is punished by social sanction. In other words it paid one to be so, for a good reputation mattered so much. We see in India how the nature of politics has altered the cost-benefit of moral behaviour. People are adapting to the new morality. When we talk of adaptation in biological terms, conscience was designed to maximise fitness- that is to exploit the local environment in the name of genetic self-interest but success in social settings is alien to natural selection. Human status has often little to do with raw muscular power. The range of things that can bring status is different in different cultures.

We can put it this way: Human beings are designed to assess their social environment, and having figured what impresses people, perform an act, and having found out what people generally disfavour, avoid that action. Some drives and emotions may not be erasable-like lust and jealousy. Our thrust for approval, assignment of blame and credit mark the evolutionary importance of self-advertisement. In modern society the common enemy may be obscured but instead we have 'common interest'. 'Even a six years old will discreetly elicit opinions about the local bully before mounting a challenge'.

(Wright, 1994, p. 288).

The nature of our brains

We must have an understanding of our brain and its limitations as the source for our behaviour. Neuro-biologists view our brain as the result of evolution where the earlier forms are contained within the later formations. According to neuro-biologist, Paul D. MacLean (1990) we have a 'triune brain'- a reptilian core, a paleo-mammalian brain and a neo mammalian brain. Repression and the unconscious mind are the products of millions of years of evolution, well developed long before civilisation. Our skull holds three distinct evolutionary strata that have formed upon the older, larger layer before it like an archaeological site. The three strata operate like three interconnected biological computers with its own special intelligence, its own subjectivity, its own sense of time and space and its own memory. Each of these is connected by nerves to the other two, but each seems to operate on its own brain system with distinct capacities.

The old mammalian brain residing in the limbic system is concerned with emotions and instincts, feeding, fleeing and sexual behaviour. Physiologically, it includes the hypothalamus, hippocampus and amyglada. It helps determine valence, for example whether you feel positive or negative towards something.

In Buddhism, this is referred to as vedena that is what gets your attention, unpredictability and creative behaviour. The old mammalian brain has vast interconnections with the neo-cortex so that the brain functions are not either purely limbic or purely cerebral but a mixture of both. MacLean[.http://www.kheper.net/topic/intelligence/

MacLean] feels that that the lowly mammalian brain tends to be the seat of our value judgements instead of the more advanced cortex. The cortex is divided into left and right hemispheres- the left controls the right side of the body while the right controls the left side. The right has more characteristics of spatiality, abstract thought, musicality and artistic ability. The left is more linear, rational and verbal. There are critics of the triune hypothesis. Elaine de Beaufort (1996) a neurologist and psychotherapist in her work, "Crossing The Threshold of The Unconscious- into the Basic Brain" argues that although the deepest brain is similar to reptilian formation, and although some of the basic activities seem reptilian such as repetition, imitation and deception, there are subtleties not conveyed by words. When we take into account the link between the spinal cord, including the afferent/efferent nervous system and extending to the openings of our skin, the brain with the link to the spinal cord, the brain would seem to convey that much larger implications are involved. The following is an extract from her work:

"In the formation of the basic brain we make our first appearance as human life. This is our first brain of basic rhythm, of motion, of reaction and action. This brain exposes to the earth through our skin which no longer slithers on the earth but which nevertheless clings to whatever is near. We note the ways we invent to be on the earth; to control and dominate by using our work, our children, god and finally ourselves." (p. 1)

It is in this first brain when other brains no longer function, that we know we are alive....What kind of consciousness is here?

- the continuous beating of the heart
- the continuous breathing of the lungs
- the continuous expansion and contraction of the brain.

Beauport further explains the link between the spinal cord and our deeper part of the brain. She contends that whether we are conscious or not of the energy we call 'self' or energy that surrounds us, life goes on. Whether caused by physical damage to the brain, the normal rest periods of sleep, or just lack of awareness the basic brain continues to filter energy. As long as there is life, energy still passes through the basic brain. To access this energy according to her, we need the following abilities:

(i) the ability to enter into the rhythms of what is happening.

(ii) the ability to create parameters and to dissolve them when they are appropriate.

(iii) the ability of neutral observation of ourselves and all that surrounds us.

(iv) the ability to move toward and away from in tandem with life closest to us which is the freedom of the deepest brain. She places a lot of emphasis on the function of the spinal cord which serves as the channel to filter incoming vibrations. Our spinal cord links us to the outside world by means of our nervous system which is continually receiving impulses from our muscles and skin.

(v) although we are used to think of our skin as something that covers our body, it is more appropriate to see it as our interface with the environment.

I might add that Indian Ayurvedic medicine treats the skin not as a mere cover but as an important communicating device.

Our understanding of consciousness is to focus on this process of reception from the environment. She suggests that consciousness involves observing, studying and taking into account the context in which we live. If we are to be behaviourally intelligent we must observe our reactions and interactions not as owner but as neutral observer. The reticular formation connects the major nerves in the spinal column and the brain. It sorts out the impulses that constantly assault the brain. When these are registered in the emotional part of the brain, we become conscious of our feelings; when they get registered in the neo cortex, we think, imagine, relate and intuit. It is possible that we do not become conscious of much of this energy until later- all of a sudden we may get it. The subtle and neutral movement of the brain can explain our anti-social routines, rituals and values that become deeply entrenched. We have a constant wave motion- this is solidified in the physical structure of the spinal cord and carries the vibrations. This basic energy that is carried has a pleasurable sweetness. The essence of control is entering the basic rhythm.

I have sumamrised the essential conclusions of the author here and omitted the physiological description of the brain, spinal cord and so on. What is interesting is how closely our Indian philosophy and meditative practices predate these findings. In deep meditation, there is suspension of thought and one enters the 'basic brain' and is conscious of only vibrations and a feeling of bliss. The different states of consciousness is explained in our yoga tradition as: sleep, dream, wakefulness, and 'turiya' the fourth state which is the deep experience of the energy of the basic brain. Taitreya Upanishad describes our sates of consciousness in the following way:

> swapna: dream; jagara: wakefulness; sushuptum: sleep; turiya: the fourth state beyond all these three. Secondly, the connection of the spinal cord to many neural events and its importance too, has been elaborated in our yogic tradition as 'kundalini'. Unfortunately, Beauport nowhere refers to Eastern knowledge. There are many verses in the Vedas and the Upanishads that explore consciousness. Likewise Ayurveda emphasises skin massage as significant for health. The skin here is not seen as 'mere covering of the body' but a transmitter of sensations important for healing.

To come back to Darwin

According to Darwin, the human species is a moral being because the human is capable of comparing his past and future actions or motives and of approving or disapproving them. We are moral in this sense that we have the technical capacity for leading a truly examined life: we have self awareness, foresight and judgement. According to Wright (1994), we are not designed for chronically subjecting ourselves to a true and bracing moral scrutiny and adjusting our behaviour accordingly. We are potentially moral animals but are not naturally moral animals.

Reference

1. [One can recall the story of wolf children. Two children abandoned by a parent as infants were tended by a wolf. They could walk on all four-using their hands and legs and could not speak. After discovery, they were taught slowly to become like a human.]

Chapter - 4

Mind in Buddhist Psychology

From my reading of Tibetan Buddhism I draw some conclusions about how our minds work-their strength and weakness. Buddhism emphasises experiential knowledge rather than dogmas. It holds systems of concepts and sets of postulates to be hypotheses that would require to be tested. Buddhist psychological methods of observation, study human potentialities as they now exist as well as how to develop them to realise those potentialities. Ye-shesr Gyal-mtshen in his book "The Necklace of Clear Understanding" (1975) gives a succinct account of what he calls 'The Way'. (p. xv, introduction):

> "The way is a short-term for the fact that man controls his future because of his ability to perceive, to know and to order what he perceives and know. This ability is dynamically active at this and every moment...The way begins with the accumulation of all that is necessary for man's intellectual and spiritual growth and merges into the linkage of what has been learned with further growth, which were results in a new vision or fresh perspective, enabling the beholder to see more easily, the intrinsic nature of the universe and of himself...The way involves the whole personality, which is as much body as it is feelings, the mind and set of values and interpretations."

The Buddhist approach to the mind is to see the connection between the mind and mental event. While seeing belongs to the mind, seeing its specific characteristics belongs to a mental event. However, mind and mental event arise together. The mental events that operate in the wake of every mind situation are: feeling tone, conceptualisation, directionality, rapport and ego centric demanding. The text goes on to categorise what are positive mental events and how to cultivate them. These eleven positive mental events are listed as: confidence, trust, self respect, decorum, non-attachment, non-hatred, non-deludedness, diligence, alertness, concern, equanimity and non-violence. In other words, these are the essential constituents of ethical behaviour. Although generally, there are many wrong views, what happen to be invidious are those that deny the cause –effect of events and actions. Thus, the approach lays down the foundation for ethical behaviour and the necessity for abjuring dogmas and opinions and clinging to ideologies. In this context the basic emotions which obstruct true understanding of things as they actually are include attachment, anger, arrogance, not being aware of one's full capability, indecision and opinionatedness. The Buddhist 'way' offers us away of how we can realise our human potential and experience both growth and health.

Life exacts a price for less than full participation. Our survival depends on our willingness to work with the full power of our minds and hearts in this journey of life. What will bring balance and harmony to our lives is to participate fully in life.

Tharthang Tulku (1991) emphasises that the Buddhist ethic relates to our links with other lives, human and non-human. Balance is achieved by our ways of relating to our own nature as well as that of others. The virtues discussed in previous paragraphs are precisely those that promote well being in terms of all of us such as–integrity, honesty, loyalty, responsibility and co-operation.

Human behaviour poses many mysteries. Themes we have to solve are:

- distinguishing between behaviour and the mental organ governing it,
- remembering that the mental organ, not the behaviour is what natural selection designed,
- remembering further that these organs must have led to adaptive behaviour to the environment of their design since that is the only reason natural selection ever designs mental organs,

- remembering that the human mind is incredibly complex, that it was designed to yield an array of behaviour, depending on all kinds of subtleties of circumstances and the array of behaviour it yields is tremendously expanded by the unprecedented diversity of circumstances in the modern social environment.

Philosophy, Metaphysics, Ethics and Human Development

Philosophy has grappled with what makes us human. What is so special about us? What is the purpose of our lives? Is this purpose realisable only by certain rules broadly called ethics? There are different ways of understanding ourselves and our place in the universe. Paul Davis, a renowned theoretical physicist regards human beings who are part of this world as creative beings, in consonance with the creative cosmos where self-organisation is the fundamental feature (Davies, 1987). Jostein Gaarder (2003) the Norwegian philosopher, well versed in Eastern philosophy and Sanskrit concludes that as thinking human beings we are created to bear 'witness' to the magnificence of the universe and we owe a great responsibility for sustaining this cosmos.

Biology offers the most striking example of self-organisation in living systems. Take the astonishing ability of an embryo to develop from a single strand of DNA via an exquisitely well orchestrated sequence of formative steps into an exceedingly complex organism. Many self-organising systems are also dissipative. They are open and not closed. They exchange energy, entropy and material with the environment. They are not static; they are processes that retain a measure of identity and at the same time they are in a state of continual flux. (Davies, 1987). After all coming to think of it you and I have within us, each cell dying and regenerating all the time and so in what sense is there an unchanging "I"? Living systems are part of complex systems of an array of interconnected sites.

It is being increasingly recognised that political, legal, economic changes do not go deep enough. By themselves they will not bring about penetrating changes in human culture and behaviour (Singer, 1979). Becoming a human being really is the prime issue of our time but on a scale never encountered before. Singer's book was published in 1980 and 1990 as second and third edition. Capra (1992) wrote about the Tao of physics. He asserts that both physics and metaphysics lead inexorably to the same knowledge. The Tao of Physics is an exploration between modern physics and eastern mysticism by Fritj of Capra (1975). His book has been published in 43 editions in 23 languages. He struggled to reconcile theoretical physics with Eastern mysticism. The book lucidly analyses the tenets of Buddhism, Hinduism and Taoism to show the striking parallels with latest discovery in cyclotrons. Capra seeks an integration of mathematical world view of modern physics and the mystical visions of Buddha and Krishna. However, his theory is now not accepted by mainstream science. Quantum Mysticism is a set of metaphysical beliefs and associated practice that seeks to relate consciousness, intelligence, spirituality and mystical world views to the ideas of quantum mechanics and its interpretations. This theory first appeared in Germany in 1920's. Edwin Schrodinger and Weiner Heisenberg were leading Quantum Physicists.

Mani Lal Bhaumik (2005): "Code Name God's central thesis in his book" is that the discoveries of modern physics can be reconciled with the great truths of the world religions, when these truths are viewed as elements of what Aldus Huxley called Perennial Philosophy. Bhaumik finds strong support in advance physics and cosmology for the Neo Platonic notion of "One" (identified as the source) and conjectures that this existential source may reside in what is known as quantum vacuum state and be in some manner co-eternal and co-equal with human consciousness. Bhaumik's book is an autobiography chronicling events in the author's life in tandem with revealations that accompanied them and a contemplation on the astounding implications of quantum physics. The surprising discovery of quantum physics that the primary source of everything in the universe is present in each minutest stitch of the fabric of space of this immensely vast cosmos, empowers us to ponder the One Source of all creation. Bhaumik's portrayal of a higher power embedded in the fabric of the universe and responsible for its continuing existence and operation is consistent with his reliance of the highly technical and mathematical intricacies of quantum field theory. Today many do not believe that Quantum theory has anything to do with consciousness. Quantum mechanics is the study of the very small. It is the body of scientific principles that explains the behaviour of atoms and subatomic particles. Quantum means the minimum amount of physical entity involved in interactions. The uncertainty principle means that the more closely one pins down one's measurement – such as the position of the particle, the less precise is another measurement pertaining to the same particle such as its momentum must become.

We have seen how various disciplines have tried to make sense of what makes us human. What makes us special? How does the human brain function? These are questions addressed by various scholars given in brief in the above passages.

Chapter - 5

Contribution of Buddhist thought to the Notion of 'Human'

Buddhist thought articulates the notion of our interconnectedness extremely well. Some principles of Buddhist Philosophy are briefly recalled here to illustrate their bearing on ethics and human development. The idea of 'Dependent- Origination' and the pervasiveness of 'Impermanence' is the essence of Buddhist thought. This resonates well with the earlier cited views of physicists and biologists on the unity of life. Buddhist notion of dependent origination demonstrates the inter-relatedness of everything. This is explained in the exposition of "Pratityasamutpada". (Sankaranarayan & Deshpande ed., 2007)

"This is like this because that is like that. Because you smile, I am happy. This is like this therefore that is like that. And that is like that because this is like this". This is called dependent co-arising. Suppose you and I are friends. My sense of well being, my happiness depends very much on you and your well-being and happiness, depends on me. I am responsible for you, and you are responsible for me. Anything I do wrong, you will suffer and anything you do wrong I will suffer. Therefore, in order to take care of you, I have to take care of myself. (Sogyal, 1988)

What does this mean for our idea of human development? It is to understand and behave in a way that realises that human development has this ethical basis of interdependence of the individual human being with other human beings, with other living systems and to this world in general that we know and live in. It stipulates the basic conditions for sustainable development that includes ecology, reducing the kind of inequality that fosters injustice, exploitation and oppression of others. The manner in which we treat animals, plants, other resources of this earth as though they exist only for us, leads to destructive development and un-sustainability in the long run, because we ignore our connectedness. When we destroy forests, we affect climate, water, land and animals. Then, tigers lose their habitat and elephants stray into cropland. Within a century mankind has exterminated thousands of species what in earlier times took many millions of years for extinction of species. How do we realise this oneness? The Buddha had a special way of understanding the object of our perception. In order to understand you have to be one with what you wish to understand. You cannot stand outside of something to contemplate it. You have to be one with it- this is called non-duality. Perception is very important for our well-being and must be free from emotions and ignorance, free from illusions. Knowledge can be an obstacle. If we take one thing to be true and cling to it, even if truth itself comes in person and knocks at our door, we will not open the door.

Impermanence

If you want to know the truth about life and death, you must reflect on this: there is only one law in the universe that never changes- that all things change and that all things are impermanent. Looking deeper into impermanence, we find another message, one that opens our eyes to the fundamental nature of the universe and our extraordinary relationship to it. If everything is impermanent, then everything is empty. Modern physics corroborate this. Within the atom, there are vast emptiness, which means what seems substantial lack any lasting, stable and inherent existence and all things when seen and understood in their true relation, are not independent but interdependent with all other things. The Buddha compared the universe to a vast net woven with countless variety of jewels each with a countless number of facets, each jewel reflects in itself, every other jewel in the net and is in fact one with every other jewel.

Think of the wave in the sea. Seen in one way, it seems to have a distinct identity, an end and a beginning, a birth and a death. Seen in another way, the wave itself does not really exist but it is just the behaviour of water, "empty" of any separate identity but "full" of water. So when you think about the wave, you come to realise that it is something made temporarily possible by wind and water and that it is dependent on a set of constantly changing circumstances. You also realise that every wave is related to every other wave.

When we say "empty" we have to understand empty of what? Nothing has any inherent existence of its own- this absence of independent existence is what we call "emptiness". Think of a tree. It looks like it has a distinct identity. When you contemplate it dissolves into a subtle set of relationships that stretches across the universe; the rain falls on its leaves; the wind that sways it, the soil that nourishes it, all the seasons and the weather, moonlight and sunlight. Everything in the universe helps to make the tree what it is; that it cannot at any moment be isolated from anything else and that every moment in nature is subtly changing. Buddhists refer to this phenomenon of connectedness as 'inter-being'.

Modern science speaks of the extraordinary range of inter-relations. Ecologists know that a tree burning in Amazon rain forest alters in some way the air breathed by a citizen in Paris, that the trembling of a butterfly's wings in Yucatan affects the life of a fern in Hebrides. Between a mouse in place A and a distant mouse in place B there is morphic resonance. Rupert Sheldrake first propounded this idea in 1981. It was republished in 1985 and subsequent editions have been brought out in 1988 and 1991. Biologists have uncovered the complex dance of genes that create personality. Each identity is composed of a swirl of influences. Even our smallest, least significant thought, word and action have real consequences. The fear that impermanence awakens in us, that nothing is real and nothing lasts drives us to ask "if everything dies and changes then what is really true? Is there something behind appearances, infinitely spacious, something in which the dance of change and impermanence takes place? Is it the deathless and unending nature of 'mind' or consciousness"?

Buddhist ideas about the nature and role of human being and her/his destiny is so much part of the Indian tradition that has influenced so many regions of this world and continues to do so.

The Buddha attaches much importance to the mind of man. He says, "Our nature is outcome of what we have thought. It is dominated by our thoughts. It is made up of our thoughts. If a man speaks or acts with an evil thought, sorrow (suffering) follows him as the wheels follow the feet of the ox that draws cart. If he speaks or acts with a pure thought (pure mind), that is, without hatred and evilness or wickedness, happiness accompanies him like a shadow" (Dhammapada,1998).

It has been taught to us since our childhood that we should love our neighbours, the people around us. But what do we see around? We do not love truly. The neighbours do not love truly. Not only your neighbours but your own people at home, your brothers and sisters also do not love truly. When one does not love in true senses, how can one expect the world to love truly? The true home of love is heart and mind. Man's mind, heart must be pervaded with love. Buddha says, "Enmities are never ceased by enmities. They are ceased only by love. This is the eternal law" (Dhammapada, 1-5) That, by love the enmities can be ceased, vanished, wiped out from the face of this earth, is the greatest truth. The Buddha told this truth more than two thousand five hundred years ago. This truth cannot be refuted or wiped out in any time in any part of the world. A human being is aware of this truth, but it is painful to realise so that she/he does not put it into practice.

In the teaching of the Buddha, there have been many things supplying world needs. There are both democracy and science. (Omvedt, 2003; Illiah, 2001). What is needed is the systematic linking of these two. Buddha himself proclaimed to the world "The Centre of my Dhamma is man and the relation of Man to another in his life on the Earth." His Dhamma is not 'Dharma', now used to signify religion or faith. In religious faith there is a binding of a human being to something higher called 'God'. This is not true of the idea of Dhamma. As a matter of fact the Dhamma itself is highest. It consists of four components.

Happiness of mind

Perfection in human conduct.

Duty for duty's sake, not for the sake of me or mine.

Goodwill maintained towards others and others towards us resulting into Universal goodwill.

When we look around the world and view the condition of people we are struck by the sad thought that there is no proper unity amongst the people that inhabit this world. In every department of life, in every sphere of human activity, there is conflict and jealousy and there is no thread to all, the lessons of virtuous conduct *(sila)*, that leads to a tranquility (*samadhi*) gradually, which step by step graduates into wisdom (*panna*) and culminates in deliverance (*vimutti*), that is (*nibbana)*. So in the dhamma of Buddha, the perplexed one finds clarity, the distraught finds solace and disheartened one finds hope and courage. (Sogyal, 1988)

Chapter - 6

The Notion of Dependent Origination

The right way of knowing Buddhism is through understanding its core premise of *'Pratityasamutpada'* or the theory of dependent origination is a crucial theory contributed by Buddhism to the world of Philosophy. According to Buddhist Dictionary, the dependent origination is "the doctrine of the conditionality of all physical and psychical phenomena, a doctrine which, together with that of impersonality (*anatta*) forms the indispensable condition for the real understanding and realisation of the teaching of the Buddha." It shows the conditionality and dependent nature of that uninterrupted flux of manifold physical and psychical phenomena of existence.

Buddha himself has said to Ananda that profound, is this dependent origination and profound does it appear. It is through not understanding, not penetrating, this law that this world resembles a tangled ball of thread, a birds nest, a thicket of sedge or reed, and that man does not escape from the lower state of existence, from the course of woe and perdition, suffering from the round of rebirth.

The linguistic formation is : Prati – I + yap = Pratitya being gone again and again; sam – ut – pad + ghan = samutpada becomes thoroughly originated. The Principle of Dependent Origination refers to a significant interpretation in sprouting the life of an animate being and that is liable to death. In other words, the problem of the life in respect of a living animate being, including that of human kind is involved in the aforesaid Principle of Dependent Origination. According to the teaching of Interdependent Co- Arising, Cause and effect co-arise (*samutpada*) and everything is a result of multiple causes and conditions. The egg is in the chicken and the chicken is in the egg. Chicken and egg arise in mutual dependence. Neither is independent. Independent Co-Arising goes beyond our concepts of Space and Time. "The one contains the all." The Buddha expressed Interdependent Co-Arising very simply: "This is, because that is. That is not, because this is not. This comes to be, because that comes to be. This ceases to be, because that ceases to be."

In the sutras, this image is given: "Three cut reeds can stand only by leaning on one another: If you take one away, the other two will fall." For a table to exist, we need wood, a carpenter, time, skillfulness, and many other causes. Each of these causes needs other causes to be. The wood needs the forest, the sunshine, the rain and so on. The carpenter needs his parents, breakfast, fresh air and so on. And each of those things, in turn, has to be brought about by other conditions. If we continue to look in this way, we will see that nothing has been left out. Everything in the cosmos has come together to bring us this table. Looking deeply at the sunshine, the leaves of the tree and the clouds, we can see the table. The one can be seen in the all and the all can be seen in the one. One cause is never enough to bring about an effect. A cause must, at the same time, be an effect - the idea of a first or only cause, something that does not itself have a cause, cannot be applied.

Pratityasamutpada has both negative and positive features, viz. darker and brighter shades. The negative aspect indicates man's helplessness in drifting away in the endless stream of cause and effect. He is mercilessly enslaved in the clutches of karma. Change is the law of nature according to Buddhism. Whether we like it or not, whether we know it or not, things change every moment. This momentariness causes suffering. Madyamikas known as *sunyavada* is mentioned in Mahayana. The term '*Sunyavada*', has a negative connotation of the non-existence of substances and in terms of positive reference, it implies the ever changing flux of *samsara*. As applied to experience, *sunyata* means the ever changing state of phenomenal world. It is reality in the sense that there is nothing concrete or individual. It is empty and distinct from *samvriti,* which is said to be real. It is not absolute non-being. In Mahayana sutra it is explained in terms of microcosm and macrocosm. When all are enmeshed in samsara, they all struggle upwards together, evolving towards something higher. It gives the sense that the whole universe is a seamless integrated whole, of which man is part and parcel. It gives all beings, a feeling of at 'homeness', in the very nature. The existential loneliness and being forlorn will then be driven away and a kind of fellow feeling that will be cultivated among all the humans.

This law is not based on axioms as the laws in Euclid's geometry, nor is it based on intellectual inference observing phenomena happening in the outside world as Newton's law of gravitation. It is a product of direct experience which man has by looking within himself with a mind free from defilements. The laws applicable in geometry and physics are different from the law of Pratityasamutpada as the latter unlike the former applies to the world where man's will is important as it is the driving force. For realising the truth of this law, one is required to experiment not in the outside laboratories. Besides, one has to develop one's body and mind i.e., insight and concentration to realise this law operating within. In short, one has to drive out defilements from one's mind in order to be fit to experience the truth of this law. For proving the laws of geometry and gravitational laws one need not necessarily be a man free from defilements. Persons having defilements like anger, hatred and jealousy can make experiments and prove those laws in the laboratories but they cannot experience how the law of dependent origination works.

Our living in society is based on the principle of "Man Is Friend And Brother of Man". We have to educate ourselves in the spirit of freedom, equality and humanism, so that we become sincere and constant supporters of peace and friendship. The universal brotherhood cannot be achieved by any religion unless peace is contemplated and achieved. The peace cannot be achieved unless unity is achieved, as one cannot control the horse unless he holds the reign firmly with all his fingers. Unity lies in freedom, equality, morality, compassion and removal of suffering and injustice. Buddhism not only preaches but practices these principles. To enjoy a life of values one has to recognise the existence of other human beings, that is, one has to acknowledge the fact that every man is born into a social order. This order begins with the family as the Buddha also lived in, but it is actually as extensive as the human race. The social order, with its many sub-systems, provides the setting and main condition of the individual's existence. Yet an individual, a unique product of Nature, influences, modifies and makes it an abode worthwhile to all human beings. (Jatava, 1998, pp. 64-65).

Humanity is a world family. The world societies/states now depend very much on each other, as the world has become smaller and more interdependent, as a result of rapid technological advances. International trade and commerce are closely interconnected. Without a sense of universal brotherhood- 'Vasudhaiva Kutumbakam'- a world family is just not possible. Without an understanding and belief that we are really a part of one big family, we cannot hope to overcome the dangers to our very existence. It is the awareness about the law of interdependence that brings liberty, equality, fraternity, peace and happiness. (Chitkara, 2002, p. 1)

In a world torn by tension, conflict, fundamentalism and threat of nuclear war, inter faith dialogue and co-operation between spiritual leaders is a good augury. Such a step can help prevent wars, check religious fundamentalism, enforce disarmament leading to peaceful co-existence among different nations. Nuclear power can be used in medicine. It can also be used to erase cities. It is wrong to expect scientists to make our decisions for us. Our whole range of experience is like the skin and scientific method is a boiler suit that we put on for special tasks. But inside we are men and our decisions are made by the whole of mankind and scientists in their common humanity are involved in these decisions as well. We have a map and in spite of this, as in all voyages, we may often enter uncharted seas. But the navigators can be none other than ourselves. "We, mankind, contain the possibilities of the earth's immense future and can realise more and more of them on condition that we increase our knowledge and our love." (Chitkara, 2002, p. 6) Interdependence is a fundamental law of nature.

The need for a sense of universal responsibility affects aspects of modern life. Interdependence, of course, is a fundamental law of nature. Not only myriad forms of life, but the most subtle level of material phenomena, as well, is governed by interdependence. All phenomena, from the planet we inhabit to the oceans, clouds, forests and flowers that surround us, arise in dependence upon subtle patterns of energy. Without their proper interaction, they dissolve and decay. Ignorance of interdependence has not only harmed the natural environment, but human society as well. Instead of caring for one another, we place most of our efforts for happiness in pursuing individual material consumption. (Chitkara, 2002, p. 16)

The truth is that higher than even inter-dependence is the state of inter-harmony, or inter-agreeableness. In dependence, there is little dignity, in inter-dependence, there is genuine self respect- it is only in the social order where this mutual harmony, or mutual agreeableness, is the guiding principle of social and individual relationship, the true freedom is obtained for men. But only he can be agreeable who in his own being is independent. The meaning of freedom is freedom to be in harmony with others. It is the freedom to summon one's inherent physical, mental, emotional and spiritual powers in the service of one's own self and of others. This, then, is the meaning of dharma; and dharma is the link which binds the individual and the social in integral unity of humanness. Body, mind, intelligence and the soul – these four makes up an individual. But these are integrated. We cannot think of each part separately. Progress of men means simultaneous progress of the body, mind, intellect and soul of man. (Chitkara, 2002; pp. 173-174; 2003, p. 154)

Chapter - 7

The Essence of Mahayana Buddhism

In Sanskrit, it is 'mahajnana' which in Pali is 'mahayana'. Mahayana Buddhism is one of the main existing schools of Buddhism and a term for classification of Buddhist philosophies and practice. It was founded in India. It is used in three main senses: as a living tradition, the larger of the two major traditions of Buddhism today, the other being Theravada. As a method of classification of Buddhist philosophies, Mahayana refers to spiritual motivation (also known as Bodhisatvayana. According to Vajrayana scheme of classification of practice paths, Mahayana refers to one of the routes to enlightenment- the other two being Hinayana and Vajrayana. Although the Mahayana movement, traces its origins to Gautam Buddha, scholars believe it originated in India in the first century CE. Mahayana became the mainstream movement in India in the fifth century CE since that is when Mahayanic inscriptions started to appear in the epigraphic records of India. In the course of its history, it spread throughout East Asia (China, Japan, South Korea, Vietnam) and Tibet. Tibetan Buddhism worldwide is the result of diaspora.

Doctrine: Doctrine means a loosely bound bundle of many teachings. It has a large religious and philosophical structure and sees itself as penetrating more profoundly Buddha's Dharma. Mahayana de-emphasises the ideal of release from suffering and the attainment of Nirvana found in early Buddhist schools. The fundamental doctrines of Mahayana were based around the possibility of universal liberation from suffering for all beings (and hence the 'great vehicle') and the existence of Buddhas and Bodhisattvas embodying Buddha nature. Some Mahayana schools simplify the expression of faith by allowing salvation to be alternately obtained through the grace of the Buddha Amitabha by having faith and chanting to Amitabha. This devotional style spread in East Asia where spiritual elements traditionally relied upon were: chanting of Buddha's name, of mantras, of reading the sutras and mysticism. In China, it is combined with Zen.

Early Buddhist triad: Bodhisattva Maitreya

The Buddha

Bodhisattva Avalokitesvara

Bodhisattva means symbol of altruistic excellence.

Later Mahayana Buddhism had four main types: Madhyamaka, Yogacara, Thathagathagarba and Buddhist Logic. *Madhyamaka* and *Yogacara* became the most important schools.

From the fifth century onwards, Mahayana was a strong movement in India, owing to support from the Gupta Dynasty. It then spread to South East Asia, Central Asia, China, Korea and Japan. Buddhism disappeared from India in the eleventh century and lost its influence. *Teravada* gained prominence in Sri Lanka from where it spread to South East Asia. Zen Buddhism discarded the concept of Bodhisattvas and instead focused on meditation.

Philosophy of Mahayana: universalism (every one can become a Buddha) bodhichitta (focus on realisation) compassion (through transfer of merit) transcendental immanence (immortal Buddha principle).

Mahayana does not consider the attainment of 'arahat' as final. Nirvana without reminder is followed by Nirvana with reminder. The Buddha first achieved enlightenment first and then at death maha – parinirvana. (This is illustrated in cave 26 at Ajanta)

Early schools felt that Maitreya will not attain nirvana while Gautam Buddha's teachings still exist. Buddha principle or Buddha nature means 'luminous mind'. This is the concept of 'agamas'. The Tathagata –garbha does not represent a substantial 'self' or 'atman'. It is an expression of emptiness or *sunyata* and represents the potentiality to realise the ultimate personality possible. *Sunyata* does not mean nihilism.

'*Sunyata*' is a characteristic phenomena arising from the fact (as observed and taught by Buddha) that the impermanent nature of form means that nothing possesses enduring identity. Buddha's spiritual teaching, insight into the emptiness of phenomena is an aspect of the cultivation of insight that leads to wisdom and inner peace. The importance of this is especially emphasised in Mahayana Buddhism and receives more positive explication in Thathagatha sutra.

The Buddhist concept of 'emptiness' is difficult to grasp. The *Sunyata* doctrine declares that we attain emancipation by emptiness. Emptiness is a liberating insight in *Theravada* tradition, rather than a philosophical view. Understanding emptiness is subordinate to the ultimate goal of liberation. Another view is that in advancing personal growth, it is not metaphysics but phenomenology that is required. Metaphysical view is irrelevant or harmful if its intrinsic emptiness of the fruits of an unskillful act provides a rationale for performing that act.

The Heart Sutra declares that the 'skandas' which constitute our mental and physical existence are empty in their nature and essence. This emptiness which is at the same time not different from the kind of reality which we normally ascribe to events, it is not nihilistic emptiness that undermines our world but a positive emptiness which defines it.

Nagarjuna provided the most philosophical formulation of '*sunyata*'- emptiness is the hallmark of all phenomena and is a natural consequence of dependent origination.

Nagarjuna put forward a bold argument regarding *nirvana* and *samsara*. If all phenomenal events (that constitute *samsara*) are empty then they are empty of any compelling ability to cause suffering. Nirvana is not something added to *samsara* on any process taking away from it (that is removing the enlightened being from it). In other words, 'nirvana' is simply samsara rightly experienced in the light of a proper understanding of the emptiness of all things.

Buddha said, 'By cultivating non-self in connection with *thathagarbha* (which is the indwelling immortal Buddha element) and having continually cultivated emptiness, suffering will not be eradicated but one will become like a moth in a flame'.

In the Tibetan version, *nirvanic* liberation (*moksha*) by contrast is said to open up a realm of "utter joy, permanence, stability and eternity" unlike the *Madhyamaka* a version of philosophy which holds it to be negative. However, the Tibetan version of Mahayana pari nirvana is positive. The concept of sunyata or voidness has been rejected by critics of Buddhism. Hiriyanna (2009) gives a good explanation of this concept and Buddha's denial of a 'self' was not negative as it sounds.

According to Robert E. Thurman (2000): Voidness does not mean 'nothingness' but rather that, things lack intrinsic reality, intrinsic objectivity, intrinsic identity or intrinsic referentiality. Lacking, such static essence does not make them not exist -it makes them thoroughly relative."

The concept of 'emptiness' is very subtle, difficult to understand even for Buddhists. Emptiness refers to emptiness of inherent existence. According to Madhyamaka (which means middleway) - central tenet of Mahayana, ordinary beings misperceive all objects of perception in a fundamental way. This misperception is caused by the psychological tendency to grasp at all objects of perception as if they really existed as independent entities. Ordinary beings believe that such objects exist out there, as they appear to perception- they are perceived and thought to exist from their own side exactly as they appear.

One of the most important philosophical insights of Buddhism comes from this theory of emptiness. At its heart is the deep recognition that there is a fundamental disparity between the way we perceive the world, including our own experience within it. In our day to day experience, we tend to relate to the world and to ourselves as if these entities possessed self-enclosed, definable, discrete and enduring reality. For example, if we examine our own conception of selfhood, we will find that we tend to believe in the presence of an essential core to our being, which characterises our individuality and identity as a discrete ego, independent of the physical and mental elements that constitute our existence. The philosophy of emptiness reveals that this is not only a fundamental error but also the basis for attachment, clinging and the development of our numerous prejudices. According to the theory of emptiness, any belief in an objective reality, grounded in the assumption of intrinsic, independent existence is simply untenable. All things and events, whether material, mental or even abstract concepts like time, are devoid of objective, independent existence. To intrinsically possess such independent existence would imply that all things and events are somehow complete unto themselves and are therefore self contained. This would mean that nothing has the capacity to interact with or exert influence on any other phenomena. But we know that there is cause and effect- turn a key in the car, the starter motor turns the engine over, spark plugs ignite and fuel begins to burn. Yet in a universe of self contained inherently existing things, these events could never occur. So effectively, the notion of intrinsic existence is incompatible with causation: this is because causation implies contingency and dependence, while anything that inherently existed would be immutable and self enclosed. In the theory of emptiness, everything is seen as merely being composed of dependently related events; of continuously interacting phenomena with no fixed, immutable essence which are themselves in dynamic and constantly changing relations. Thus, things and events are empty in that they can never possess any immutable essence, intrinsic reality or absolute 'being' that affords independence. Buddha was well versed in the existing philosophical systems. Perhaps he drew also from Advaita philosphy. According to Advaita, this world consciousness is consciousness of the difference between things, of taking such difference to be ultimate and believing that the multitude and variety of things are also ultimate. Reality consciousness is the opposite of this plurality consciousness. Modern physics talks of oneness.

Chapter - 8

Individual and Society Interface

Much of ethics has to do with the individual human being's relation to society or what we may call the collective within which she/he operates. According to selected Buddhist texts we reproduced above, the beginning has to be made within one self through a strong commitment to ethics. We live in society and there are different interests of different people that have to be reconciled.

Morality is woven into the fabric of Buddhist teachings and there is no major branch or school of Buddhism that fails to emphasise the importance of the moral life.

(Keown, 2005) The scriptures of Buddhism speak eloquently of virtues such as non-violence and compassion and the Buddhist version of the 'Golden Rule' counsels us not to do anything to others we would not like done to ourselves. Though there are a variety of Asian traditions, there is a common moral core underlying the divergent customs, practices and philosophical teachings of the different schools. This core is composed of the principles and precepts and the values and virtues expounded by the Buddha in the fifth century BCE.

The ultimate foundation for Buddhist ethics is Dharma. The underlying notion is of a universal law which governs both the physical and moral order of the universe or natural law which enshrines the principle of order and regularity seen in the behaviour of natural phenomena along with the idea of a universal moral law. Every aspect of life is regulated by Dharma, from the successions of the seasons to the movements of the planets and constellations. Dharma is caused by not under the control of a supreme Being–

Even the 'gods' themselves are subject to its laws. In the moral order Dharma is manifest in the law of karma, which governs the way moral deeds affect individuals in present and future lives. Living in accordance with Dharma and implementing its requirements is thought to lead to happiness, fulfillment, and salvation; neglecting or transgressing, it is said to lead to endless suffering in the cycle of rebirth (*samsara*). We may not believe in rebirth but the seeds of suffering felt by a person is communicated to her/his progeny. A boy unloved by parents suffers and his vulnerability is reflected in the way he is unable to love others.

The doctrine of karma is concerned with ethical implications of Dharma, in particular those relating to the consequences of moral behaviour. Karma is not a system of rewards and punishments meted out by God but a kind of natural law akin to the law of gravity.

It is not what happens to a person like good and bad luck. The literal meaning of karma is action in Sanskrit but karma as a religious action is concerned not with just any action but with actions of a particular kind. Karmic actions are moral actions and the acts consequent upon them. Buddha stated, that it is intention (*cetana*), that is karma; having willed, one acts through body, speech or mind.

Moral actions are unlike other actions in that they have both transitive and intransitive effects. The transitive effect is seen in the direct impact moral actions have on others, for example, when we kill or steal, someone is deprived of his life or property. The intransitive effect is seen in the way moral actions affect the agent. According to Buddhism, human beings have free will and in the exercise of free choice they engage in self determination. In a real sense individuals create themselves through their moral choices. By freely and repeatedly choosing certain sorts of things, individuals shape their character and through their character, their futures. Even within the course of a single lifetime, particular patterns of behaviour lead inexorably to certain results.

Not all the consequences of what a person does are experienced in the life time in which the deeds are performed. Karma does not determine precisely what will happen or how any one will react to what happens and individuals are always free to resist previous conditioning and establish new patterns of behaviour. (YE-she-r Gheyal-mtshan, 1975)

What then makes an action good or bad? For Buddha, it is largely a matter of intention and choice. Actions, which are motivated by greed (*raga*), hatred (*dvesa*) and delusion *(moha*) are bad (*akusala*), while actions motivated by their opposites- non-attachment, benevolence and understanding (*kusala*) making progress towards enlightenment is not simply a matter of good intentions; they must find expression in right actions which are basically those that are wholesome and do no harm to either oneself or others. Buddhist tradition expresses ethical requirements in the form of duties rather than rights.

There are five precepts (pancasila), then eight, then ten. Rules must not only be followed but they should be for the right reasons. The most important virtues are: (i) *dana* (generosity), (ii) *ahimsa* (non- violence), (iii) *karuna* (compassion).

The four Brhma viharas: (i) metti (*maître* or loving kindness); (ii) *karuna* (compassion) and (iii) sympathetic joy (*mudita*) and (iv) equanimity (*upekka*) [Pali words].

Mahayana Buddhism did not reject the ethical teachings of early Buddhism but subsumed them under an expanded framework with three levels. 1. moral discipline (*samvarasila*), 2. cultivation of virtue (*kusala-dharma-sangrahaka-sila*), 3. altruistic conduct (*sattva-artha–kriya–sila)*. An important innovation in Mahayana was the notion of 'skillful means' (upaya kausalya). Mahayana had this understanding that the early texts were guidelines and not literal rules. Buddhist moral teachings emphasise self discipline.

The Four Noble truths:

Dukkha: All existence is suffering

Samudaya: Suffering is caused by craving

Nirodha: Suffering can have an end

Marga: The way to end suffering is the Noble Eightfold path

The Eigthfold path and its three divisions:

1. Right View (Insight prajna)
2. Right Resolve

3. Right Speech
4 Right Action (Morality - sila)
5. Right livelihood
6. Right Effort
7. Right mindfulness (samadhi)
8. Right meditation

Vinaya : Dharma Vinaya (doctrine and discipline) was the whole body of Buddhist teaching and practice relating to the monastic order (sangha) which existed as a just another sect within a broader community of wanderers and teachers know as sramanas.

The perfections are: Generosity (*dana*); morality (*sila*); patience (*ksanti*); perseverance (*virya*); meditation (*samadhi*).

There is emphasis on compassion in Buddhism. Compassion is not pity and it is not a passive attitude. On the other hand it is an active principle. It is as Boff (1986) says: It is about not viewing things only from one's own view but to place oneself in the others' situation. It is what makes one come out of one's own sphere and entering into that of the other to suffer with the other, to walk with the other and to build life in synergy with the other in empathy. (p. 90)

Conclusion: Buddhism's essential approach

Buddhist moral teachings are grounded in the cosmic law of Dharma rather than commandments by God. These are revealed by enlightened teachers. In leading a moral life one becomes the embodiment of Dharma and anyone who lives in this way and keeps these precepts can expect good karmic consequences such as happiness in this life and a good rebirth in the next and eventually attainment of Nirvana. Mahayana Buddhism places a special emphasis on service to others.

Even if one discards the belief in rebirth, our actions do affect others who come after us.

Chapter - 9

Eastern and Western View of Ethics

Western ethics has three categories: descriptive ethics, normative ethics and meta-ethics.

The distinction between morality and ethics is that morality denotes the standards and values of a society as they exist on the ground while ethics refers to the critical analysis of those values by people such as philosophers.

The nature of Buddhist ethics:

it is both egotistical and altruistic because it seeks good for oneself and others

it is mainly absolutistic

it is objective

it is neither deontological or teleological but a form of virtue ethics

it is naturalistic

it is cognitive

While Buddhist ethics is concerned with the specifics of individual conduct, engaged Buddhism focuses on larger questions of Public policy such as justice, poverty, politics and environment. Clearly there is a connection between them and it is no coincidence that both these disciplines have arisen at roughly the same time when Buddhism encounters the West. "Socially Engaged Buddhism" has become important in modern Buddhism worldwide. Buddhism is often perceived to be individual and passive in its approach to social problems. This view might have been promoted by Western scholars of the nineteenth century. Socially engaged Buddhists have now led active protests, utilising American and European forms of social protest and active social involvement. The promotion of engaged Buddhism owes much to the Vietnamese monk Thich Nhat Hanh emphasising awareness in daily life, social service and social activism. While engaged Buddhism applies to human rights issues, non-violence and environmental concerns, it also has an impact on the lives of individual Buddhists. [Thich Nhat Hanh, 2008]

Is there a Buddhist perspective to deal with contemporary problems? Though it has no ecclesiastical authority, it is possible to have a consensus among different schools.

Buddhist view on ethical issues has a modern origin. Buddhism is seen as more eco-friendly - encourages a path of harmonious integration with nature and as fostering identification of mutual respect within the natural world as humans can be reborn as animas and vice versa. Buddhist world view suggests a much closer kinship between species where by different forms of life are inter-related in a profound way. Yet, it is not the same as the modern 'green' values or animal rights. Human beings remain the primary focus- values belong to humans and nature is to be protected for their sake. There is prohibition of meat eating, though not mandatory for everyone in practice.

Is Buddhism same as deep ecology and eco-feminism?

The notion of 'dependent origination' has some problems for ecology as it does not distinguish between say carbon dioxide and nuclear waste. Eco-feminism sees men as responsible for exploitative conduct towards nature. A better way of establishing a basis for ecology in Buddhism is to emphasise the ecological aspects of the ethical virtues which are the central element in Buddhism-loving kindness, compassion, non-violence and wisdom promote ecological concern by their very nature.

Chapter - 10

Deep Ecology

The attempt in this essay is to understand the location of human beings in nature and what it means to our goal in life. For this purpose various philosophical schools were briefly recalled. Modern environmental science further seeks to affirm our connection to the natural world and how our destiny is linked to how we negotiate that connection.

Deep ecology is a somewhat recent branch of ecological philosophy (ecosophy) that considers human kind as an integral part of its environment. It is a body of thought that places greater value on non-human species, eco-systems and processes in nature than established environmental and green movements. Deep ecology has led to a new system of environmental ethics. The core principle of deep ecology is the claim that like humanity, the living environment as a whole has the same right to live and flourish. Deep ecology describes itself as 'deep' because it persists in asking deeper questions concerning 'why' and 'how' and this is concerned with the fundamental philosophical questions about the impact of human life on one part of the eco sphere, rather than a narrow view of ecology as a branch of biological science and aims to avoid merely utilitarian environmentalism which it argues is concerned with conservation of the environment so that it can be exploited for human purposes.

Development of the concept of deep ecology

The phrase 'deep ecology' was coined by the Norwegian philosopher Arnes Naess. In 1990, he helped give it a theoretical foundation. For Arne Naess, if ecological science is concerned with facts and logic alone, it cannot answer ethical questions about how we should live. For this we need ecological wisdom. Deep ecology seeks to develop this by focusing on deep experience, deep questioning and deep commitment. These constitute an interconnected system. Each gives rise to and supports the other, while the entire system is what Naess would call an ecosophy- an evolving but constant philosophy of being, linking and acting in the world that embodies ecological wisdom and harmony.

Naess rejected the idea that beings can be ranked according to their relative value. For example, any judgement on whether an animal has an external soul, whether it uses reason, whether it has consciousness (or indeed higher consciousness) have all been used to justify the human as superior to other animals. Naess states that from an ecological point of view' the right of all forms of life to live is an universal right which cannot be quantified. No single species of living being has more of this particular right to live and enfold than other species. This metaphysical idea is in Warwick Fox's (1986, 1990) claim that we and all other beings are aspects of 'a single unfolding reality'. As such deep ecology would support the view of Aldo Leopold's book "A Sand County Almanac" (1949) where he says that humans are plain members of the biotic community. Deep ecology supports Leopold's 'Land Ethic'- a thing is right when it tends to preserve the integrity, stability and beauty of the biotic community. It is wrong when it tends otherwise. Daniel Quinn in his Ismael (1995) showed that an anthropocentric myth underlies our current view of the world and a jellyfish would have an equally jelly centric view.

Deep Ecology offers a philosophical basis for environment advocacy that may in turn guide human activity against perceived self-destruction. Deep ecology and environmentalism hold that eco-system can absorb only limited change by humans or dissonant influences. Further both hold that the actions of modern civilisations threaten global ecological well-being. Ecologists have described change and stability in ecological systems in various ways including homeostasis, dynamic equilibrium and flux of nature. Environmentalists contend, that massive human activity has pushed the biosphere far from natural state through reduction of biodiversity, climate change and other influences. As a consequence civilisation is causing mass extinction. Deep ecologists hope to influence social and political change through their philosophy. To the extent that ecology deals with human beings relation to nature, it is in accord with Buddhist philosophy that speaks of our relatedness to all living and non-living things.

Chapter - 11

Scientific View and Spiritual View

Naess (1973) and Fox (1990) do not claim to use logic or induction to derive their philosophy directly from scientific ecology but rather hold that scientific ecology directly implies the metaphysics of deep ecology, including its ideas about the self and further, that deep ecology finds scientific underpinnings in the field of ecology and system dynamics.

In their book, Devall and Sessions (1995) described a series of sources for deep ecology. They include the science of ecology itself and cite its major contribution as the discovery in a modern context that 'everything is connected to everything else'. They point out that some ecologists and natural historians in addition to their scientific viewpoint have developed a deep ecological consciousness, some political consciousness and at times a spiritual consciousness. This is a perspective beyond the strictly human viewpoint, beyond anthropocentrism. Among the scientists who were forerunners are Rachel Carson (1962), Aldo Leopold (1949), John Livingston (1994), Paul B Elrilch (2013) and Barry Commoner (1976) together with Frank Fraser Darling (1971), Eugene Odum (1993) and Paul Sears (1980).

Rachel Carson was a marine biologist whose book "Silent Spring (1962) recorded the detrimental effects on environment and the natural world with the use of pesticides. Aldo Leopold's book on "Sand Country Alamanc" (1949) (mentioned earlier in this text) alerted his country on the need for expansion of ethic to include non-human members of the biotic community. He argued that the land ethic simply enlarges the boundaries of the community to include soils, water, plants, animals collectively. From 'homo sapiens' as conquerors humans must become plain member earth and undertake ethical care of the land community. John Livingston's famous book "Rogue Primate" (1994) was an exploratory treatise on human domestication. He loved nature with every cell in his body. Every where he looked he found nature suffered at our hands and that the human species has lost its way. Somewhere in prehistory, we eroded our own wilderness and with that our stake in preserving the wild for itself. He pointed out that in our struggle to survive, we distanced ourselves from hunger, parasites and predators. In the process, we ended up destroying almost everything natural about ourselves-the good and bad. In human society, ways of 'Doing' supplanted ways of 'Being'. Livingston won the Governor's award for his work. Paul Elrich gave us the gloomy prediction that the collapse of our global civilisation cannot be avoided because of our rapacious use of the earth's resources. Barry Commoner (1976) was a biologist who wrote on Nature, Man and Technology, formulated four abiding principles of life on earth that we need to understand.

1. Everything is connected to everything else.
2. Everything must go somewhere.
3. Nature knows best. Human technology is detrimental to the nature system.
4. There is no such thing as free lunch.

Frank Fraser Darling was not only an English farmer but an ornithologist beginning with 1938 when he wrote "Wild Country. A Highland Naturalist's Notes and Pictures" He wrote many books. His 1971 work, "A Conversation on Population, Environment and Human Wellbeing" stands as a classic text on our responsibility to safeguard the source of our well being. To Eugene Odam we owe the term eco-system. He developed ecology as a discipline. His 1993 book, "Ecology and Our Endangered Life Support System" sounds a warning to our careless depredation of the wealth of this earth. Paul Sears's book (1980) 'Desert on the March' which indicated how the Dust Bowl was created in mid-West in the USA had a profound impact on policy. A new branch of study called 'eco-psychology' deals with the relationship between human beings and the natural world through the application of ecological and psychological principles. The approach is to develop and understand ways of expanding the emotional connection between individuals and the natural world. Do we not as city dwellers seek to holiday in places which have natural beauty without our built environment- the mountains, rivers, canyons and so on? Why do people engage in environmentally destructive behaviour? Though this tends to be addictive, positive reinforcement can be induced by the emotional fulfillment through our innate instinct to connect emotionally with nature during our evolutionary adaptation to the natural conditions that human species evolved to inhabit.

Ecology has been a constant factor in advancing many societies. Some knowledge of management and use of natural resources was implicit in indigenous communities.

Today ecologists are those with more advanced scientific knowledge and have gone beyond life sciences. Because of rapid changes in our knowledge base and the more complex organisation of human societies, the functional knowledge of their environment by indigenous societies is of limited value at the present juncture as they lack the modern theory rooted in modern science. As Bandhyopadhyay (2015) argues, Western scientific paradigm is able to absorb practice and enrich theory, where ecological sciences are drawing on physics and mathematics, for example, in analysis of global warming and climate change. The ability of modern science of European roots to theorise and combine theory with practice has greater chances of evolving future strategies for eco-system management.

Today's environmental approach has a basis on social philosophy. John Searle an American philosopher dealt with philosophy of language, philosophy of mind and social philosophy. He received 'Mind and Brain' prize in 2006. In his book 'Intentionality' he defined intentionality as the power of minds to be about, to represent, to stand for things, properties and states of affairs in the world. His Essay on the Philosophy of Mind (1983) speaks of the set of abilities, capacities, tendencies and dispositions that humans have and that are not in themselves intentional states. When someone asks us to cut the cake, we know we have to use a knife; when someone asks us to cut the grass, we know we need a lawnmower. In his book, "Rediscovery of the Mind" (1992) he argues that from early influential views on behaviourism, modern western philosophy has vainly tried to deny the existence of consciousness. In his work on intentionality he parodies several alternative theories. No one would think of saying that having a hand is just being disposed to certain sorts of behaviour such as grasping. Sears maintains that philosophy has been trapped by a false dichotomy – on the one hand, the world consists of nothing but objective particles in fields of force yet on the other hand, consciousness is clearly a subjective experience. Both versions are true: consciousness is a real subjective experience caused by the physical process of the brain.

Critics like Daniel Dennet (1991) dismisses subjectivity as unscientific as science is held to be 'objective'. Perhaps the goal of science is to establish and validate statements which are 'epistemically' objective–whose truths can be discovered and evaluated by any interested party but are not ontologically objective. We must distinguish between brute facts, for example, the height of a mountain from an institutional fact like a baseball game. Our notions of rationality are flawed. In any decision situation, we see a gap between our reason and our actions. Much of our rational deliberation involves adjusting our (often inconsistent) patterns of desires to decide between outcomes, not the other way round. Rationality is not a system of rules but more of an adverb. We see certain behaviours as rational, no matter what its source is and our system of rules derives from finding patterns in what we see as rational. The advantage of science according to Karl Popper is its quality of falsifiability. Unlike belief systems where one cannot prove or disprove faith, in science, when new data or finding comes in, the earlier one is 'falsified'.

Popper (1934/2004) in his book, "Philosophy of Science" gives a good summary of his ideas.

It is easy to obtain confirmations or verifications for nearly every theory- if we look for confirmations. Confirmations should count only if they are the result of risky prediction- that is to say if unenlightened by the theory in question, we should have expected an event which was incompatible with the theory an event which would have refuted the theory. Every 'good' scientific theory is a prohibition; it forbids certain things to happen. The more a theory forbids, the better it is. A theory which is not refutable by any conceivable event is 'non-scientific'. Irrefutability is not a virtue of a theory (as people often think) but a vice. Every genuine test of a theory is an attempt to falsify it or refute it. Testability is falsifiability but there are degrees of testability; some theories are more testable, more exposed to refutation than others; they take it as it were, greater risks Confirming evidence should not count except when it is the result of a genuine test of theory; this means it can be presented as a serious but unsuccessful attempt to falsify the theory. In such cases 'corroborating evidence'. Some genuine testable theories, when found not to be so, are still upheld by admirers - for example, by introducing some auxiliary assumptions or by re-interpreting theory in such a way that it escapes refutations. Such a procedure is always possible, but it rescues the theory only at a price of destroying or at least lowering its scientific status. To sum up: the criterion of scientific status of a theory is its fasifiability, or refutability or testability.

Deep ecology had faced critics and supporters. As some scientists dismissed ecology as subjective Dregson and Alan (1995) and Devall and Sessions (1985) provided a scientific source for deep ecology. This development can be traced to the 'new physics', which shattered Descarte's and Newton's earlier vision of the universe as a machine explainable in terms of simple linear cause and effect. Instead of providing merely a turning point for their characterisation of how new physics leads to metaphysics and ecological views of inter-relatedness, deep ecology can be made into a framework for human societies. (Capra, 1982). Capra's view aligns with the Buddhist notion of nature in constant flux and the idea that observers and the observed are separate is an illusion. Devall and Sessions also credit American poet and social critic Gary Snyder (1990, 1991, 1999) who with his devotion to Buddhism and Native American studies as well as the outdoor and alternative social movements, was part of major voices of wisdom that helped in their evolution of their own ideas. The scientific vision of the 'Gaia' hypothesis was also an influence on the development of deep ecology. Gaia is the image of the earth as a whole organism.

Spiritual Approach

The central spiritual tenet of deep ecology is that human species is a part of the Earth and not separate from it. A process of self-realisation, or 're-earthing' by an individual enables one to intuitively gain an ecocentric perspective. The notion is based on the idea that the more we expand the self to identify with others (people, animals, eco-system), the more we realise ourselves. Transpersonal psychology has been used by Warwick Fox to support this idea. (op. cit) In relation to Judeo Christian tradition, Naess (1989) offers the following criticism: 'The arrogance of human stewardship as found in the Bible consists of the idea of human superiority which underlies the thought that we exist to watch over nature like a highly respected middleman between the creator and creation'. This theme has been expounded in Lynn Townsend White Junior (1967). As a professor of medieval history at Princeton and Stanford, he traced the historical roots of the present day ecological crisis. In his 'Medieval Technology and Social Change' (1962), he argued that the role of technology in human affairs has been neglected. The Bible asserted man's supremacy and his domination over nature and is responsible for establishing anthroprocentricism. Christianity makes a distinction between Man formed in God 'image' and the rest of creation which it held has no soul, no reason and is inferior to Man. It is this perception that lies at the root of our ecological crisis. An alternative view of nature in the Christian tradition is offered by St. Francis of Assessi, who spoke of the equality of all creatures in place of the idea of man's domination over creation.

Experiential

Drawing upon Buddhist tradition, Joanna Macy worked as an anti-nuclear activist in the USA. She found that one of the major impediments confronting the activist's cause was, the presence of unsolved emotions of despair, grief, sorrow, anger and rage. The denial of these emotions led to apathy and disempowerment. We may have intellectual understanding of our interconnectedness but Western Culture robs us of emotional and visceral experience of that interconnectedness which we had as small children but which have been socialised out of us by an anthroprocentric, alienating culture.

Through her work 'Despair and Empowerment Work' and 'Work that Reconnects', Macy and others have been taking deep ecology into USA and Europe. (Macy, 1990)

Principles of Deep Ecology

Proponents of Deep Ecology believe that the world does not exist as a resource to be freely exploited by humans. Bender (2003) and Diamond (2005) in his book "Collapse" had documented how societies that neglect the need to preserve their environment court disaster. Panmore (1974) had emphasised man's responsibility towards Nature. The ethics of deep ecology holds that a whole system is superior to its parts. They offer an eight tier platform to elucidate their claims.

1. Well being and flowering of human and non-human life on earth have value in themselves intrinsic/inherent. These values are independent of the usefulness of the non-human world for non-human purposes.
2. Richness and diversity of life forms, contribute to the realisation of these values in themselves.
3. Humans have no right to reduce the richness and diversity except to satisfy vital human needs.

The flourishing of human life and culture is compatible with a substantial decrease of the human population. The flourishing of non-human life requires such a decrease in human population. Present human interference with the non-human world is excessive and the situation is rapidly worsening. Policies must therefore be changed. These policies affect basic economic, technological and ideological structures. The resulting state of affairs will be deeply different from the present. The ideological change is mainly that of appreciating life quality which would include among other things the following: learning to dwell in situations of inherent value, rather than adhering to an increasingly higher standard of living. There will be profound awareness of the difference between big and great. Those who subscribe to the foregoing points have an obligation directly or indirectly to try to implement the necessary changes. (Katz, 2000) essays on the philosophy of deep ecology elucidate many of these principles.

Movements

In practice deep ecologists support decentralisation, the creation of eco regions, the breakdown of industrialism in its current form and an end to authoritarianism.

Deep ecology is not considered a distinct movement but as part of the Green Movement. The deep ecological movement can be defined as those within the Green Movement who hold deep ecological views. Deep ecologists welcome the label 'Gaian' or 'Green' (including commitment to peace). Deep ecology has had a broader general influence on the Green Movement by providing an independent ethical platform for Green parties, political ecologists and environmentalists. The philosophy of deep ecology help differentiate the modern ecology movement by pointing out that the anthroprocentric bias of the term 'environment' and reflecting the idea of humans as authoritarian guardians of the environment. For something to require rights and protection intrinsically it must have interests.

Interest in Nature

Deep ecology is criticised for presuming that plants, for example, have their own interests. Deep ecologists claim to identify with the environment and in doing-so criticise those who they claim have no understanding what the environment's interests are. When deep ecologists give to nature an interest such as growth, survival and balance, they assume that these are also in our human interest. The idea that earth is endowed with wisdom, implies that given freedom, wilderness and life forms when left alone, emit moral qualities. It has also been argued that species and eco-systems themselves have rights. Can humans in governing their own affairs be somehow immune from this assumption to understand the interest of the rest of humanity? While the deep ecologist critic would answer that these interests are ultimately observable solely from the logical application of the behaviour of the life form, which is the same standard used by deep ecologists to perceive the standard of interest of the natural world.

Is the notion of Deepness valid?

Deep ecology is criticised for its claim to be deeper than alternative theories, which by implication are shallow. However, despite repeated complaints about the use of the term, it still enjoys wide currency. 'Deep' has an attractive resonance for many who seek to establish a new ethical framework for guiding human action with respect to the natural world. It may be presumptuous to assert that one's thinking is deeper than others. When Arne Naess coined the term 'deep ecology' he compared it unfavourably with shallow environmentalism which he criticised for its utilitarian and anthroprocentric attitude and for its materialist and consumer oriented outlook. Against this is Naess's own view that the depth of deep ecology resides in the persistence of its interrogating and questioning, particularly in asking 'why' when faced with initial answers.

Eco Feminist response

Both eco feminism and deep ecology put forward a new conceptualisation of the self. Some eco feminists such as Mart Keel (1990) argue that self-realisation and identification with all nature puts too much emphasis on the whole, at the expense of the independent being. Eco feminists contend that their concept of the self (as a dynamic process consisting of relations) is superior. Eco feminists would also place more emphasis on the problem of androcentrism, rather than anthropocentrism. India also has eco feminists, but their ideas will be taken in a later section when we come to contemporary Indian views and social conflicts generated by developmental processes.

Social ecologists such as Murry Bookchin (1987) claim that deep ecology fails to link environment crises with authoritarianism and hierarchy. Social ecologists believe that environmental problems are firmly rooted in the manner of human social interaction and claim that an ecologically sustainable society could still be socially exploitative. Deep ecologists reject this argument that ecological behaviour is rooted in the social paradigm. According to their view this is an anthroprocentric fallacy and they maintain the converse of the socio-ecologist's objection is also true in that it is equally possible for a socially egalitarian society to continue to exploit the earth. There are parallels here in Indian history too, of primitive tribes' interaction with nature which was not necessarily benign.

Misunderstanding Scientific Information

Daniel Botkin (2000) has likened deep ecology to its anti-thesis, "the wise use movement', when he says they both misunderstand scientific information and then arrive at conclusions based on their misunderstanding, which are in turn used as justification for their ideologies. Botkin begins with an ideology that is political and social in focus. Elsewhere though, he asserts "deep ecology must be taken seriously in the debate about the relationship between humans and nature because it challenges the fundamental assumptions of Western philosophy. Botkin also criticised Naess's restatement about the balance of nature idea and the contradiction between his argument that all species are morally equal with his disparaging description of the idea of pioneering species.

Is Shallow View Superior?

Writer William Grey Walter (1961) believes that developing a non-anthroprocentric set of values is a hopeless quest. He sees an improved 'shallow view' is not their concern about the well being of humans, but they do not consider enough in what their well being consists. We need to develop an enriched, fortified anthroprocentric notion of human interest to replace the dominant short term. He was influenced by the Russian physiologist Pavlov. He improved the EEG (elctro encephalograph) to study brain waves. In 1961, he discovered contingent negative variation- according to which a negative spike of electricity appears in the brain half a second prior to the person being consciously aware of the movement. This brings into question the notion of consciousness or freewill and should be considered as part of a person's overall reaction to events.

Fritj of Capra in his book, "The Turning Point" (1983) has a very well reasoned critique of economic theory and the present pre-occupation with economic growth. In the following paragraphs we summarise his main conclusions. It was at the beginning of the nineteenth century that economists systematised the discipline to give it the aura of a science. Later some tried to shift the focus away from the earlier view of welfare as material production to the subjective criteria of individual, pleasure and pain (utility). Pareto (1843-1923) added his theory of optimality by which social welfare would be increased if the satisfaction of some could be increased without diminishing that of others.

Economic efficiency uses monetary values. The valuations that count are the valuations of those who are willing and able to support theirs. This requires private ownership of resources and unrestricted rights to exchange ownership. Those who believe that particular resources could be more valuably employed in some other way can raise the price and bid them away from current use; they can indicate their preferences by offering money. Currently in India agricultural land is being bid away for industrial uses and a special land acquisition bill is now in the parliament. It is not a question of consent or fair compensation but also the importance of agriculture which is languishing for lack of public support. Food security demands that we ensure the production and distribution of food crops. Monetary values cannot be a guide here. There are many key resources used by communities that do not require payment –like clean air, pure water. These decisions have a moral basis.

Nuclear energy and nuclear power pose hazards which political imperatives ignore at our own peril. There have been accidents which are warnings. Sane vices have consistently argued for renewable energy like solar, wind and biomass. Capra while detailing these truths points out that soil requires returning organic matter to the earth. The emergence of big corporations, the Food industry processing food and using energy for this, are unsustainable. Likewise medical education and research have distorted health priorities. These warnings are worth heeding if humanity has to survive and safeguard its source of life, namely the health of the Earth. To quote Capra (1975): "The new vision of reality we have been talking about is based on an awareness of the essential inter-relatedness and interdependence of all phenomena- physical, biological, psychological, social and cultural. [p. 285]. In the history of the Earth, the co-evolution of microcosm and macrocosm is important. In this process, sexual reproduction and emergence of consciousness were critical. Capra asserts that mind is the essence of being alive. Individual human minds are embedded in the larger mind of social and ecological systems. As our physical resources become scarcer, we have to invest more in people. Many spiritual traditions vouch for ecological wisdom.

There have been attempts to create co-operative society. The Utopian Socialists set up factories and mills according to humanitarian principles, reduced working hours, increased wages, provided recreation, insurance, housing and funded co-operatives. These bold ventures failed against the onslaught of a hostile profit seeking economic environment. Other visionary voices like that of John Stuart Mill and Marx provided criticism of capitalism as it developed. Mill clearly saw the political nature of distribution of wealth in society and drew attention to the ethical choices involved. Marx demonstrated the exploitative nature of capitalism. The USA., today is a leading figure of capitalism because its industrial work force was transient, migratory could not build worker solidarity as in Europe to prepare the ground for socialism.

One of the characteristic of present day economies is a singular obsession with growth. The very conceptual basis of economic theory excluded social and environmental costs.

As our resource base diminishes, raw materials and energy must be extracted for more degraded sources. To deal with economic phenomena from an ecological perspective economist must revise their basic concepts in a drastic way. GNP as a measure of a country's progress has to be replaced by a holistic conception of human welfare and well being. This involves a profound change in our value system-replace material enrichment by human enrichment; restore our spiritual traditions, keep a balance of work and leisure.

Links of Ecology with other movements

Parallels have been drawn between deep ecology and other movements, in particular the animal rights movement and Earth First. Peter Singer's 1975 book, "Animal Liberation" critiqued anthroprocentricism and put the case for animals to be given moral consideration. This can be seen as part of the process of expanding the prevailing system of ethics to wider groups. However, Singer has disagreed with the deep ecologist's belief in the intrinsic value of nature, separate from questions of suffering, taking a more utilitarian stance in his books, "Practical Ethics" (1979, 1993). He is considered a prominent bioethical philosopher. The reverence of nature finds echoes in recent times. (Zimmerman, 2005). Our responsibility for nature as the source of our lives becomes apparent when we realise the adverse effects that our thoughtless use and abuse of nature has landed us in. (Panmore, 1974)

Carl Sagan (2011), the cosmologist pleads for us to take care of each other and take care of the earth. Voyager 1, on Feb 14, 1990 left our planetary neighbourhood for the fringes of the solar system. Voyager 1 was 6.4 billion kms away and approximately 32 degrees above the ecliptic plane. Caught in the Centre of scattered light rays,- a result of taking the picture close to the Sun, earth appears as a tiny point of light- a crescent only 0.12 pixels in size. Sagan gives a poetic rendering of our earth.

"Look at this. That is us. That is home That is here. That is us. On it every one you love, every one you know, every one you ever heard of, every human being who ever was, lived out their lives... The earth is a small stage in a vast cosmic arena. Think of the rivers of blood spilled by all those generals and emperors so that in glory and triumph they could become the momentary masters of a fraction of the dot. Think of the endless cruelties visited by inhabitants of one corner of pixel and the scarcely distinguishable inhabitants of some other corner; how frequent their misunderstandings, how eager they are to kill each other, how fervent their hatreds.

......Our posturings our imagined self importance, our delusion that we have some privileged position in the universe are challenged by the is point of pale light. In this obscurity, in all this vastness, there is no hint that help will come somewhere......The Earth is the only world we know so far to harbor life.......It underscores our responsibility to deal more kindly with each other, to preserve and nourish the pale blue dot, the only home we have ever known."

The feminist and civil rights movements also brought about expansion of the ethical system for their particular domain. Likewise deep ecology brought the whole of nature under moral consideration. The link with animal rights is strongest as proponents of such ideas argue that all life has intrinsic value. Many in the radical environment movement 'Earth First' appear to follow deep ecology as indicated by one of their slogans and the Wilderness Project during 1995-1997. It has also been a strong advocate of deep ecology and engaged in public debate with Murray Bookchin on the subject.

Bookchin (1987) posed a challenge to the ecology movement by espousing social ecology.

Judy Bari was another prominent Earth First exponent who espoused deep ecology. She was a union organiser. In 1988, she began protest against overcutting of timber in the Red Woods of California. The Timber workers tried to plant a bomb in her vehicle. She invited some representatives of small logging companies for a dialogue and signed an agreement with them for non-violent, non-destructive timber harvesting. Unfortunately, proposition 130 to promote this agreement was defeated in1990 but in 2002 the jury found that in her case her civil rights were violated. Sadly Judi did not live to relish her victory for she died of breast cancer in 1997.

Many Earth First actions have a distinct deep ecology theme, often these actions are ostensibly to save an area of old growth forest, the habitat of a snail or owl, even individual trees. It should, however, be noted that especially in the U.K., there are also strong anti-capitalist and anarchic currents in the movement and actions are symbolic or have other political aims. At one point, Arne Naess also engaged in direct environment action, though not under the Earth First banner, when he tied himself to a Norwegian Fijord in a successful protest against the building of a dam. Robert Greenway and Theodore Roszak (1992; 2001) have employed the deep ecology platform as a means to argue for eco psychology. Although eco psychology is a highly differentiated umbrella that encompasses many practices and perspectives, its ethos is generally consistent with deep ecology. As this theme is now fourty years, old, the field expands, continues to be re-interpreted by a variety of practitioners, social and natural scientists, humanists, eco psychologists and may change to include new perspectives.

'Our Common Future' in 1907 was the first international conference by Brundtland Commission to begin a discourse on environmental issues. Earth Summit in 1992, followed this initiative. At this conference, global issues like climate change, biodiversity, forest conservation, population control and the need to share responsibility were taken up. The conference also gave suggestions on operationalisation of the Bruntdland Commission's recommendations. Long before environmental issues became a current preoccupation and have led to many popular protests against projects that have posed hazards to environment like the opposition to the Narmada dam's height being increased, or against mining in Odisha for the displacement of people, their livelihoods and erosion of fragile natural formations like the Western Ghats and destruction of biodiversity in the bargain. Gadgil and Guha had first sounded alarm bells in their path breaking book, "This Fissured Land" (1995). Social conflicts over nature and natural resources are increasingly taking place. Gadgil and Guha noted the emergence of competing claims over forest, land, water and fisheries. They saw the environment movement as a new a face of Indian democracy, because it has posed an ideological challenge to the dominant notion of the meaning, content and patterns of development. The point is the movement is not just about protecting nature, but safeguarding the lives of many communities who tend to lose their livelihood based on a more friendly relation to natural resources without over exploitation. The Chipko movement in the 1970's in Central Himalayas where women hugged trees to save them from loggers who were thirsting for sale of timber that fetches high value in the market. The diminution of the rights of local communities over that of the state right from colonial regime has spelt disaster. This is one side of the picture. The other side is: village artisans facing lack of access to essential raw materials. In my own study among cane bamboo workers among Ratnagiri in Western Maharashtra, this loss was evident as their traditional claim with landlords gave way to commercial interest in serving the market for Mango trade and transport. The artisans traditionally wove utilitarian containers for agricultural use-winnowing trays, rice drying mats etc. The transition from subsistence agriculture to market production eroded many rights of artisans.

Environment concern in India has been active in opposing the construction of dams or hydropower projects and mining as destructive of fragile environments. Rangarajan *et.al* in Volume-I have explored critical environmental issues in India (2006). This edited book with eight chapters covers a whole range of issues, - definition of ecology, evolutionary history of man, linkages between environmental influence and human life, biomass resources and empirical issues. Technology, Development and Environment are interrelated issues. The book exposes how the problems we face today such as ozone depletion, global warming and far reaching environmental degradation are linked to the patterns of development we have ushered in. In the name of agriculture we have denuded our forests; pesticides are dumped in our lakes and rivers and our underground aquifers are going dry with excessive drawing of water through tube wells. Our natural resources have been exploited at the cost of future generations. The human species is a new entrant to a world where many forms of life have existed since its inception. The pre-industrial world, the book recalls had controlled consumption. Our reverence to nature is extolled in our ancient scriptures. Ecological development has become a necessity for our own survival. Use of heavy metals is another effect of industrialisation. The ill-effects on human health are visible in terms of high cholesterol, hypertension, atherosclerosis and so on. The use of synthetic chemicals have increased morbidity though antibiotics have saved lives from infectious diseases. However, excessive use of antibiotics have led to drug resistant bacteria.

Volume II (2012) of the Rangarajan ed. book gives a good history of environmental history of India. Pandey and Jyoti in the above book have elaborated food and feeding as one of the most important biological aspect and the first step in understanding the ecological role of fish population in an acquatic environment. In recent years, a plethora of books have emerged on the crisis in our environment. Pratap Singh and A.S. have dealt with Human Ecology and Development in India. (web site)

The earlier Government in India had an expert panel under Madhav Gadgil to advise on the impact of a intended hydropower project in Western Ghats. Its recommendations were as follows:

> "Educate the villagers about understanding the ecology around them so that they do not merely accede to the opinions of government experts. The villagers have no easy access to

information and are misguided by local politicians. 94.7 per cent of the area should be seen as ecologically sensitive."

Unfortunately, the report by the government expert Kasturirangan, ignored these wise observations and recommended proposed projects to be taken up. This government report held that Gadgil panel's conclusions over states the case about negative environmental effects. The then head of the environment ministry P.D. Raut declared that as 120 rivers originate in the Western Ghats, this is an excellent opportunity to exploit this resource by power projects.

Recent Concerns for Ecology

November 13, 2013 at a meeting organised by the Expert Panel that co-ordinated the redefinition of ecologically sensitive areas (ESA), proposed by the Kasturirangan Committee, MLAs across the political spectrum opposed the zonation of the Western Ghats regions. They feared this would halt development, affect construction, agriculture, tourism and scupper the development of the Sabari hill shrine. Only one legislator argued for restrictions on development to protect forest and maintain biodiversity. However, the House adopted the stand that only protected forests would be part of ESA. The high level working group headed by Kasturirangan had earmarked 13,108 sq. kms in 123 villages. The Kerala Sastra Sahitya Parishad had felt this would be disastrous. Both ruling and opposition parties have surrendered to the vested interest of builders. The decision to exclude settlements and agricultural land from ESA was taken to assuage the fear of farmers about losing land and livelihood. The ESA notification was under the Environment Protection Act to regulate industrial activity. The criterion adopted for ESA is unfair and went against the principles of conservation and will give a fillip to the destruction of Western Ghats said environmentalists. It will also be a setback to recovery of encroached land through legal means. [The Hindu, Sunday, August 2, 2015, page 11]

The Mines and Minerals Amendment Bill 2015, contain no provisions for consent from tribals for mining operations but strengthens the rights of private sector. The bill bypassed Grama Sabhas (Village Committees) and existing environmental laws in the name of speedy clearance. Though the 1957 Law was amended it continued to strengthen mining companies. In 1997, the Supreme Court upheld tribal rights. The Panchayat extension to tribal areas, the Scheduled Areas Act of 1996, and Forest Rights Act of 2006 were all attempts to uphold tribal rights. Recently the Supreme Court struck down the agreement reached between Vedanta, a mining company, and the State Government as it did not have the consent of tribals. In 2010, a partial recognition of the Adivasi (tribals) demand for a stake in mineral wealth, the UPA Government made an amendment to 1997 Act which said any person or persons holding an occupation or usufruct or traditional rights over the surface of the land will be allotted free shares equal to 26 per cent through Company's quota and further annual compensation as mutually agreed. However, succumbing to mining companies pressure, replaced it in 2011 by "Mines, Minerals Development and Regulation." The latest move by the present government has diluted even these provisions to favour the private sector mining companies–a blatant betrayal of tribal rights.

The struggle continues over Western Ghats towards conservation of bio-diversity. Six states which encompass the forest region–as compiled by NGO-Jhatka exposed the sham in the name of public consultation. Colonel Muthanna, President of Coorg Wild Life Society, said 30 per cent of Coorg comprises forest that gives 50 per cent inflow to Cauvery River.

Madhav Gadgil committee had given priority to Gram Sabhas but the timber lobby and builders lobby have carried the day. The local residents were unaware of ESA. There is thus total lack of transparency in the decisions. RTI queries have not been replied to either. Sand quarrying too has been approved, [The Hindu, August 7, 2015, p. 19, Friday].

Up in the North in the region of Uttarakhand, agencies are pushing for hydel power projects in the eco sensitive region. The Union Ministry is setting up new committees to over rule the previous ones. Environmentalists have been objecting to the formation of new committees as a violation of ecological principles and rights of the local people and is malafide in intent (Upadhyaya, 2015).

A comparison between the Ecology Expert panel (WGEEP) headed by Madhav Gadgil and the High Level Working Group

(HLWG) set up by the government show differences in their approach and methodology. There has been no dearth of disapprovals from a wide spectrum of political actors, from the left to the right. Let us recall the mandate of the Western Ghats Ecology Expert Panel (WGEEP) which included the following functions: (i) demarcation of the boundaries of the Western Ghats; (ii) identifying areas to be classified as Ecologically Sensitive Zones (ESZ), and (iii) making tentative suggestions for regulating these zones. Apart from these, the WGEEP also provided guidelines for the formation of Western Ghats Ecological Authority. Subsequently, the Ministry of Environment had constituted the High Level Working Group. This group's report was made available to the public on 15 April 2013. This debate highlights the age old issue of the trade off between environment and development. The GEEP report relies on the Forest Survey of India which is not detailed enough to incorporate forest cover, agricultural areas and species. The HLWG relies on Indian Resource Satellite data. Both reports assign scores to individual grids formed through satellite imagery, based on various criteria and their corresponding physical attributes. The WGEEP emphasises the regulation of forest and non-forest land use in ESZ. It recommends development of eco-tourism, promotion of biomass based industries, ban on use of genetically modified crops to preserve natural vegetation, species, regulations for transport and infrastructure as well as centralised power generation by large scale thermal plants and hydroelectric power plants. Also, it proposed a moratorium on mining and polluting industries. On the other hand, the Kasturirangan report argues that environmentally sound projects cannot preclude livelihood and economic options for the region. Neither report analyses the impact of their recommendations on peoples' livelihood. Decisions regarding the regulation of land use areas and agricultural practices, on the closure of polluting industries or imposing a moratorium on mining cannot ignore the inequalities with regard to the various perceptions of risk central to existing socio-economic divergences. What is not clear is how exactly priority will be accorded to the recommendations of expert groups vis-à-vis the various stakeholders, namely, the livelihood and income options of significant proportion of the population, the possible threat to the employment of labour, the concerns of cultivators within agricultural landscapes, the concerns of state governments and the pressures of industry. Risks and uncertainties are inevitable factors in social and economic planning and policy. Not only have the two reports not included economic parameters, they differ with respect to approaches to regulate ESZs and ESAs. So far public response to both reports have been on the whole, unfavourable. (Nagarajan *et. al.*, 2015)

Many recommendations by High Level Committees have been thrown on the wayside. For example, The Subramanian Committee constituted in 2014, reviewed the existing environmental laws:

Environment Protection Act, 1986

Forest Conservation Act, 1980

Wild Life Protection Act, 1972

Water (prevention and control of pollution) Act, 1981

The Indian Forest Act, 1927

Despite these plethora of laws, in practice, their implementation was tardy. The Committee had suggested that parliament could enact a law 'Environment Laws Management'. However, these recommendations were rejected in 2015. Among other notable recommendations were the following: (i) creating an Indian Environment Service like the Indian Administrative Service; (ii) identifying forests of no go areas in forests to ensure retention of 70 per cent of canopy cover and that protected areas are not disturbed except in exceptional circumstances; (iii) legislation to define the term forest in the Forest Conservation Act, 1980; and (iv) providing economic incentives for community participation. Unfortunately, this voice of wisdom went unheeded.

During 1970, a programme of Social Forestry was initiated. It was part of forest policy. Its main features were: tree planting in village commons, wood lots, along road, canals and railway lines (Donhaue, 2003).

Agro forestry was encouraged–to supply fuel and fodder trees. Later to supply the sports industry's need for soft wood, eucalyptus tree plantations were taken up. This was a controversial move as experts held that eucalyptus plantations led to excessive depletion of water resources. Social forestry was a good move and promised many positive outcomes. It helped greening of barren lands and restoration of degraded forests. In addition, it added income to farmers and increased employment in rural areas. At the moment no clear assessment is visible on how much of social forestry has been actually implemented. The critical importance of forests for climate maintenance is only now beginning to be realised. Trees outside forest are equally important. The destruction of forest for mega projects of power and industry would lose for us what would take thousands of years for replacement. Plantations cannot replicate ecological balance. Short sighted, rapacious raiding of earth's resources will bring only ruin to our civilisation.

In conclusion, we can say, the environment movement in India is not just about nature but equally about displacement of people, of ways of life, and fundamentally an ideological battle against rapacious development. It is also about equity and social justice.

India has a Ministry of Environment and laws to prevent damage to environment. There is a requirement that projects can be cleared only after proper assessment of the impact on nature and people that is social impact is done and the majority of the people of the area should be consulted and their concurrence is necessary before launching a project. Unfortunately, the present government has diluted many provisions in the Land Acquisition Bill, succumbing to Industry lobby. Many high level committees as well as the Supreme Court have unequivocally laid down precautions against both dumping of hazardous wastes as well as democratic procedures for people's consent along with concern for the impact on environment (Lockhart, 2015).

The Personal and Social in Ethics

Buddhist prescriptions referred to earlier are highly idealistic. There are Western philosophers who see ethics and its connection to human society somewhat differently. We believe emotions are antagonistic to ethics. Milton Frisk (2008) argues there is a relation between ethics and emotions. The main goal of ethics is making societies survive. Culture organises relationship with others. Ethics is usually seen as being polluted by emotions. On the other hand, evolutionary biology and psychology argue that human societies have a built in co-operative ethics. Ethics cannot function without some kind of feelings for society. Most of us want society to survive and dread its collapse. The social, it is felt requires dropping attachments and renouncing the personal.

The tension between personal and social requiring dropping attachments is not a correct view. Ethics is not one unified whole. There are different contexts in which it operates. For example, there is the ethic of self-care, ethics of business, ethics of nationality, ethic of the family and so on. Thus, ethics has multiple applications. It is actually a group of norms applied to different contexts. We have to look for the content within it and for the social dimension. There is no need to separate the social from all other categories of ethics because the ultimate ethics is one where the social good is preeminent. The areas to be distinguished are: (a) ethics of authenticity; (b) ethics of self care and (c) ethics of special relations. With regard to the last one, why do people treat family, children and spouses differently?

Frisk under estimates in my view the power of special relations over riding the social. In India, personal ethics conflicts with the social ethic. A lot of corruption is due to giving primacy only to the personal and familial to the exclusion of the social. Caste loyalty is another excluding category. The special set of relations as applied to one's close relations is proximal ethics.

The heart of ethics involves asking some basic questions about values and decisions. One simple way to understand ethics is to see it as the process of asking the right questions at the right time about the right thing to do. To conduct an ethical analysis is to assess our actions and decisions in the light of generally accepted understanding of what is good, valuable and worthwhile. Ethics is not an abstract academic exercise. Ethical thinking tries to answer four basic questions: (1) consequences, (2) rights, (3) justice, and (4) virtue.

Consequences: Who gains and who loses? Who is hurt, who advances, who is burdened by how much?

Rights: Who has the rights in this situation? Some rights are obvious-like the right to food, shelter and basic survival needs and the right of the innocent not to be harmed but others are less obvious like civil rights, protection and benefits. Rights are often in conflict and here ethical approach ensures that there is a modicum of ethical awareness underlying the decisions.

Justice: This has to do with fairness. What criteria are used to give preference to one side rather than another to distribute limited goods and services among possible stakeholders. In this context, in India there has been a raging controversy about reservation of jobs and in public enterprises and in public educational institutions–should it be merit, need, effort or remedying past discrimination? Amartya Sen's distinction between 'neethi' and 'nyaya' is relevant here to understand ethics as normative standards while nyaya is what the context demands on the ground. Thou shall not kill is 'neethi' but to execute a criminal who has done foul deeds and whose presence is inimical to the safety of social life may be seen as 'nyaya'. (capital punishment is anathema to the ethic of not taking another life)

Virtue: Considerations here involve seeking ethical wisdom and insight from those who are recognised as morally wise people. Developing the art of ethical questioning can ensure that our conversations with ourselves, our peers, our organisations and our institutions reflect the habit of skillful inquiry, generate lively ethical considerations and lead to good decisions and actions. (Donahue, 2003). Alas, in human history, wars and conflicts have dotted the pages and continue to do so. Some biologists believe that dominance and submission are inherent in biological life. May be so, but given thinking creatures like us, who can weigh consequences, balance is sought between annihilation of the less endowed to their assimilation in an advanced society. Popper, for example, roots for liberal democracy and an open society (Popper, 1945) as the best guarantee of social good.

Today we have a new ethic of identity that attempts to transcend that of the family. With these different sets of ethics how do we bridge them to reduce conflicts? We can solve problems up to a point. But the transition from one set to another is not smooth. One way to do so is to take the social good as the ultimate criterion. We have to device systems of governance with accountability. We have to mediate conflicts through impartial agencies. People have to learn to negotiate to balance interests. The Mahabharata is an epitome of the futility of war even for a just cause. The Pandavas were dragged in to a war to get their right to the kingdom. At the end no one really benefitted.

In economics, there is a branch called welfare economics. Pareto formulated a famous dictum called "the Pareto optimum" which says that the optimum welfare for society is achieved when actions promote welfare for all without reducing it for any. Is this possible in achieving the harmony that Frisk talks about? How do we balance conflicting interests? Frisk holds that the use of public goods can resolve disputes between different peoples' rights–such as between the boss and the worker. Would reservation in education and employment practiced in India for the traditionally underprivileged under a hierarchical caste system, be an answer to Frisk solution? In all cases the social goal remains the ultimate.

Ethics and Power

"Ethics is not a mere matter of subjective opinion. Its propositions are not specific to particular individuals but apply equally to all. They have a degree of generalisability or universalisability. Ethics is meaningful only when there is choice...Ethics deals with choice not between what is good and bad but also between different moral principles, values, ends because there can be several moral ends conflicting with each other." (Nadkarni, 2011).

Frisk (2008) notes that ethics seeks to control power but paradoxically is also adopted to serve power. There are in society peaks of power that are controlled by groups of small power to avoid sharp inequalities, to keep inequalities within bounds, to do away with pyramids of power. We use power to enforce ethics, work out norms. Power can threaten the viability of society. Social power is used to reduce unequal power. We have the judiciary for this purpose. One perspective holds that you can pursue the ethical only by moving away from power. Power can be countered by reason. Reason is not a faculty but finding out what makes an argument reasonable. If we think reason should not be corrupted by power we have to admit that reason is also embedded in power. If we wish to eliminate what we see as harmful, then we have to exercise power to do so.

Lois Dumont had propounded the idea as a reflection on the Indian caste system, that we are basically 'homo hierarchicus' (1966). The lower castes emulate the upper castes.

Dumont's idea was elaborated by sociologist, M.N. Srinivas with his idea of sanskritisation which held that lower castes try to emulate upper castes by copying their practices including vegetarianism to acquire status. (M. N. Srinivas, 1952). Dumont's studies of the Indian caste system paved the way for culturuo-logical method, closely allied to Indological approach. We forget that dominance and subordinations also exists even among other mammals. There is fight for territory and mate.

Authority is needed for enforcing ethics. We enforce the rule of law. We earlier expounded Buddhist principles of social harmony as something that has to begin with the individual identifying with others out of an understanding of our connectedness. The sharing of resources like, for example, petroleum brings this issue starkly. We have at present an unstable theory where arms race is pursued because each party is using its arsenal as deterrence of the others' power. This notion is the application of game theory. According to game theory, individuals plan moves and counter-moves by anticipating the other person's likely response. Levine (2002) explained game theory and its application in economics. What is called game theory is also known as the theory of social institutions. The three main branches of economic theory encompass decision theory, general equilibrium and mechanism of design. Game theory is essentially how persons act by gauging the other's reactions by listing the players or individuals participating.

In the game, alternative choices, available to each player is listed. Levine gives a very good illustration in the following way: Suppose two persons are partners in crime, whom the police have captured and put in separate cells. If neither suspect confesses, they go free and split the proceeds of their crime,–let us say it is 5 units of utility each. However, if one prisoner confesses and the other does not and also the prisoner who confesses testifies against his partner in order for himself to be let off free. In this case he gets the full utility for himself, that is 10 units of utility while the other prisoner who does not confess goes to prison and obtains a low utility of say -4. If both prisoners confess then both get a reduced term. If both confess, both also get convicted and get 1 unit of utility which is less advantageous than full freedom. The conclusion is no matter what a suspect believes his partner to do, it is always best to confess. Instead of 'confess', 'not confess' we refer to strategies labelled 'selfish action' and action for 'common good', we note that the conflict between pursuit of individual goals and that of common good, is at the heart of many economic and social problems. If we are all better people the world would be a better place. Why would the world be a better place? In the context of our day-to-day life, if all of us are altruistic, we might forgive criminal behaviour. However, if crime goes unpunished, more would take to crime. If on balance more crimes are committed, the world would surely be a worse place! This is known as the prisoner's dilemma. Is altruism an unsullied good in all contexts? According to philosophy good cannot exist without evil. May be these are unresolved paradoxes of human life.

We have to contextualise ethics and rationality. Did socialism fail because it expected people to behave totally altruistically? Frisk thought that may be non-monetary incentives could have been given. I think the problem really was the lack of participation by a wider group of people instead of the party–the 'van guard' doing it for them. Today we have come to the critical aspect of development as participation.

Reinhold Nebuhr (1960) admits social conflict as inevitable. He drew attention to how moral life has a double focus. One focus is the inner life of the individual and the other is the necessities of a human being's social life. As for the inner life, there is a human instinct to transcendence. The role of philosophy is not to deliver truth but keep alive the spirit of inquiry, not to stop questioning, to be sensitive to the possibility that there are other sides to any issue. There are many questions that lie beyond the legitimate horizon of science. (Kolakowski, 2009). From the perspective of society the highest moral idea is social justice. From the perspective of an individual it is altruism or unselfishness. The individual has to strive to realise her life by losing and finding herself in something greater than herself. "To be free is not merely to cut off one's chains, but live in a way that respects and enhances the freedom of others' said Nelson Mandela who fought against Apartheid (a regime of discrimination against blacks by the white settlers in South Africa (2003).

Frisk however argues that there are two moral perspectives that are not mutually exclusive and the contradiction between them is neither absolute nor easily harmonised. The highest moral insights and achievements of the individual conscience are both relevant and necessary. The most perfect justice cannot be established if the moral imagination of the individual does not seek to comprehend the needs and interests of fellow human beings. Justice by assertion destroys love. Modern society according to Neibuhr has made us conscious of the relation of human communities to each other through technology, communication and travel, international agencies, regions within nation states but it underplays the relationship of individuals within the community and hence leads to aggressive collective behaviour. The highest ideals which mankind has felt are not a luxury but a necessity of the soul. We can no longer seek the highest satisfaction of individual life at the expense of social injustice. 'We cannot build our individual ladders to heaven and leave the total human enterprise unredeemed of its excesses and corruptions'. (Neibuhr, 1960) To achieve justice for the collective, we have to employ reason. However, reason is to some degree the servant of interest, social injustice cannot be resolved by moral and rational suasion alone. Conflict is inevitable. Social conflict is part of the process of gaining social justice.

Chapter - 12

The Role of Philosophy in Development Economics

We have dealt at length on the role of ethics and the role of philosophy in determining human goals and human ends. Are there value judgements that are subjective? It is useful to make a distinction between characterising and appraising value judgements argues (Pani, 2006). When we characterise value judgements, we are in effect evaluating evidence, in order to conclude that a given characteristic is in some degree present (or absent) in a given instance. Though we do not accept this readily, such characterisation of subjective judgements are more widespread in the practice of development economics. Statistical tests are expected to tell us whether a particular characteristic exists in a population or not. But the researcher does need to make a judgement about whether she considers that evidence obtained as sufficient enough to believe that a particular characteristic exists. Should she accept a five per cent degree of significance or insist on a one per cent degree of significance? The pursuit of rigour may recommend an insistence on a one per cent degree of significance but this implies that it is better to reject a pattern that might be true rather than accept one that is likely to be false. And this in itself is a subjective judgement.

Appraising value judgements on the other hand, are evaluation. Is envisaged or actual state of affairs worthy of approval? The choice of desirable outcomes for development policy would itself involve such judgements. Development economists may be unanimous on the need to remove poverty, but the very idea that poverty is undesirable is itself an appraising subjective judgement. We hold that literacy is important but some do argue that people can get along without it. Until recently any way that was the majority situation in most parts of the world when formal learning was restricted to appointed scribes either through caste or class.

It is important that we make explicit the existence of both appraising and characterising subjective judgements, so that they can be subject to a closer scrutiny. It follows that the measures needed to evaluate the quality of appraising judgements could be quite different from those required to evaluate the quality of characterising judgement. In this context one can recall what Susan Hack refers to as 'warrantable evidence.' (Hack, 1998). If we make explicit what we consider desirable, then it is possible to gauge the moral tradition from which that judgement of desirability arises. It will then be clear whether or not the moral compass of the development economist agrees with that of society. To give an example, what kind of goods and services promote overall welfare will be a question of such value judgement. Social interest is not one set of value judgements–there are interest groups whose values conflict with each other as Neibuhr points out.

There are serious philosophical issues for economics as a practice (Chandavarkar, 2007). It is a subject of cognitive dissonance. Economic laws are best statement of tendencies. Popper (1959) rejected the inductive views on scientific method. Any theory in the empirical sciences can never be proven but it can be falsified- meaning that it can and should be scrutinised by decisive experiments. If the outcome of the experiment contradicts theory one should refrain from ad hoc manoeouvres that evade the contradiction. He replaced justificatory accounts by critical rationalism in expounding the logic of research.

Economics and philosophy are both techniques of analysis rather than bodies of doctrines. Long ago Joan Robinson called economics a box of tools (Robinson, 1962). We can analyse any behaviour or outcome from an economic angle. Hence, its canvass includes epistemology, religion, ethics, psychology and rhetoric. How do we make out what people want? Economics makes the assumption of their scale of preferences as revealed in what and how much they buy. The interface with ethics lies in the criteria of justice. The unit of measurement in terms of which a person's advantage is evaluated in assessing equity and justice can be utility (the earlier neoclassical unit) primary goods (survival needs) or capabilities of an individual that help her to be and become.

Chapter - 13

Empiricism

Empiricism is the theory of knowledge that asserts that knowledge arises from experience which is one of several competing views on how we know things. It foregrounds the role of experience and evidence especially sense perception in the formation of ideas while discounting the notion of innate ideas except in so far as these might be inferred from empirical reasoning as in the case of genetic predisposition. In philosophy of science, empiricism emphasises those aspects of scientific knowledge that are closely related to evidence especially in experiments. It is a fundamental part of scientific method that all hypotheses and theories must be tested against observation of the natural world rather than resting solely on a priori reasoning, intuition or revealation. This stance was explicitly formulated by John Locke in the seventeenth century. On the other hand, rationalism asserts that much knowledge is attributable to reason independently of the senses. This is an over simplified view. Descartes, Spinoza and Leibniz were advocates of scientific method of their day.

Rene Descartes was a French philosopher and mathematician whose book, "Meditations on First Philosophy" (1641) continues to be a standard text for western philosophy. His 'cogito ergo sum' (I think, therefore I am) is a famous quote. He was a key figure in ushering in the scientific revolution. He rejected splitting of corporeal substance into matter and form and any appeals to final ends as explanation of natural phenomena. He emphasised the use of reason to develop natural sciences. Philosophy to him was a thinking system to embody knowledge. In his discourse on method (1637), he attempted to arrive at a set of principles that one can know as true without doubt. He shifted the authoritative guarantor of truth from God to humanity. The human being is a self-conscious shaper and guarantor of their own reality. Each person can be a reasoning adult, a subject and an agent. The philosophical revolution he sparked led to anthroprocentrism and subjectivism.

Baruch Spinoza's work was translated by Gilles de Leuze in 1970. His ethics is closely related to the political psychology of his times. Consciousness experiences joy and sadness depending on whether the body encountered, enters in to composition with us or tends to decompose us. It is transitive, a continual awareness of the passage from these totalities. It is not the property of the whole and as such it has only informational value. Information can be distorted and confused by our emotions.

Gottfried Wilhelm von Leibniz (1646-1716) was a mathematician and philosopher who invented the mechanical calculators. He concluded that in a restrictive sense, our universe is the best possible one that God could have created. His theories led to analysing probabilities and their relevance to linguistics and computer science. He enunciated some basic principles such as: If a proposition is true, then its negation is false and vice versa.

Two distinct things cannot have their properties in common. Sufficient reason must be there for anything to exist, for any event to occur, for any truth to obtain. The appropriate nature of each substance brings it about that what happens to one corresponds to what happens to all others without however their acting upon one another directly. There is a law of continuity. God assuredly chooses the best. The best of all possible worlds would contain all possibilities with our finite experience of eternity giving no reason to dispute nature's perfection. Human actions flow from prior causes that ultimately arise in God, therefore are known as metaphysical certainty to God. An individual's freewill is exercised within natural laws, where choices are merely contingently necessary to be decided in the event of a wonderful spontaneity that provides an escape from predestination. His theory of monads as the ultimate elementary particles have since been overtaken by modern physics.

Scientific Usage: All evidence must be empirical, depended on evidence observable by the senses. Both social science and natural science make use of 'working hypothesis' using observation and experiment. An inductive inference from direct experience ignored the possibility of existing 'groups of permanent possibilities of sensation' that is subjective idealism. It has come to be realised that there are no finite set of statements about actual and possible sense data; the former has to be deduced from the latter. There is a failure to acknowledge an aspect of reality that goes beyond mere possibilities of sensation. For example, how do find trees growing unobserved? The phenomenonalist phase of post-Hume's empiricism ended by 1940. It became obvious that physical things could not be translated into statements about actual and possible sense data. In his treatise on human nature he examined the psychological basis of human nature (1793). [www.// en.wikepedia.org/wki/determinism – my summary]

Determinism

It is a popular misconception that determinism necessarily entails that humanity or individual humans have no influence on the future and its events. This is a position also known as fatalism. However, determinists believe that the level to which human beings have influence over their future is itself dependent on present and past. Causal determinism is associated with and relies upon the ideas of materialism and causality. Some of the main philosophers who have dealt with the issue are Steven M. Cahn, Marcus Aurealius, Thomas Hobbes, Baruch Spinoza, Gottfried Leibniz, David Hume, Baron d' Holbach, Pierre Simon Laplace, Arthur Schopenhauer, William James, Frederick Nietzsche, Albert Einstein, Neils Bohr and more recently John Searle, Daniel Dennet. B.K. Skinner's approach is non-mechanistic but probabilistic.

Marcus Aurelius, a Roman Emperor wrote during 276-28 AD many texts on meditations. A central theme of his 'meditations' is on how to analyse your judgement of self and others to develop a cosmic perspective. He argued that one has the power to strip away many superfluous troubles located wholly in one's judgement and to possess a large room for oneself embracing in thought the whole cosmos, to consider everlasting time to think of rapid change in the parts of each thing, how short from birth until dissolution, how void before birth and that after dissolution are equally infinite. He advocated finding one's place in the universe and to understand that everything comes from nature and so everything shall return to it in due course. We are part of a greater construct, thus taking a communitarian approach rather than having an individualistic perspective. We should maintain focus, without distraction, pursue strong ethical principles. The only way a man can be harmed by others is to allow one's reactions to overpower oneself. An order to logos permeates existence. Rationality and clear mindedness allow one to live in harmony with logos, rising above faulty perceptions of good and bad. Steven M. Cahn ed. (2007) "Classics of Western Philosophy" gives a useful account of the basic approaches of Western Philosophy. Western philosophy veered away from engagement with the spiritual aspects.

Nature of Determinism

Historically, there are several interpretations. There is the incompatibilists' view, which accepts free will and rejects determinism as mutually exclusive categories. The view that free will is an illusion is 'hard determinism'. The soft determinists believe that the two ideas can be coherently reconciled. Definition of free will varies. Determinism is the theory that our choices and decisions are what give rise to them as effects. It is effects that are fundamental to the theory – how it affects our lives. Causal Determinism holds that future events are necessitated by past and present events combined with the laws of nature. This has a direct relation to predictability. Scientific Determinism holds that all laws have a cause and effect and the precise combination of events at a particular time engender a particular outcome. Perfect predictability does not necessarily imply lack of determinism. Limitations on predictability could alternately be caused by factors such as lack of information or excess complexity. For example, a bomb from the air- we can predict the time the bomb reaches the ground, we also know what will happen when it explodes. Any small error in prediction might arise from our not measuring some factors, such as puffs of wind or variation in temperature along the path. Logical Determinism is the notion that all propositions whether about the past, present or future are either true or false. The problem of free will in this context is the problem of how choices can be free, given that what one does in the future is already determined as true or false. This is referred to as the problem of future contingents.

Compatibility view: Free will and Determinism can co-exist. How can we have free will if everything is determined? If we have free will how can determinism be true? In the ethical context, if the true state of the universe is determined by its past and laws of nature, then we cannot blame someone who commits a crime. Likewise if someone has accomplished some things it would appear 'he was bound to do so'. This cuts against our common beliefs that: (i) crimes should be punished and (ii) accomplishments should be praised. There are arguments for incompatibility. Whether we can cause our choices to come about in the right way or if we determine them for ourselves sufficiently or not, does determinism take away the power to choose? According to Hume, some kind of determinism is required if we want to have free will, in order to make plans or choices, for we expect the same action or cause to have the same result or effect each time– otherwise what use is free will if we never know what will come of our decisions? David Hume examined the psychological basis of human nature. According to him, desire rather than reason governed human nature. He rejected that there are innate ideas and argued that humans can have knowledge of only things they actually experience. It implies that inductive reasoning and causality cannot be justified rationally. Our assumptions in favour of these result from custom and constant conjunction with logic. He thought humans have no actual conception of the self-only a bundle of sensations associated with the self. Hume contributed to the development of logical positivism, utilitarianism and analytical philosophy.

Is there a Natural Law? Several philosophers are sceptical about the existence of natural law. What are these laws? Quantum theory is said to be in-deterministic. This is a major epistemological issue with determinism. It is claimed that the universe on a large scale is deterministic or behaves so. Determinism involves the following precepts:

This is the way things are. There are natural laws, therefore the way things will be depends on natural law. Determinism will have to apply to the whole universe and then it becomes a metaphysical idea.

Eastern Tradition

A shifting flow of probabilities for futures has at the heart of theories associated with—

Y Jing Ching's, "The Book of Changes" (1965). Probabilities take the centre stage away from things and people. A kind of 'Divine Volition' sets the fundamental rules for the working of the probabilities of the universe and human volition is always a factor in the ways that humans can deal with real world situation one encounters. If one's situation in life is a 'tsunami' one has choices–either give up or seek to survive. This is the Japanese and Chinese view. In the philosophical schools of India (Hindu, Jain and Buddhist), there is concept of precise and continual effect of the laws of karma, on the existence of all sentient beings. Karma is action or deed, that which causes the entire cycle of cause and effect. This cycle is samsara.

Modern Perspectives on Determinism

We have the Big Bang theory as the beginning of the universe, but where did the compressed universe come from? Can something come from nothing? The philosophical argument of the Big Bang theory is that it triggered every single action, including mental thought through systems of cause and effect. According to generative philosophy free will is an illusion. We experience free will due to the generation of infinite behaviour from the interacting finite deterministic set of rules and parameters. Thus, the unpredictability of the emerging behaviour from deterministic processes leads to a perception of free will, even though free will as an ontological entity might not exist. Many mathematical models are deterministic. At atomic scale, paths of objects can be predicted only probabilistically. Some hypothesise that there might be hidden variables. At the macro scale the universe appears deterministic. Intrinsic to the debate concerning determinism is the idea of First Cause. This is the approach of logical positivism.

Biological Determinism: Holds that biological factors such an organism's individual genes as opposed to social or environmental factors completely determine how a system behaves or changes over time example: taste in music, committing murder, writing poetry etc. Biological determinist looks at only innate factors such as genetic makeup ignoring the role of custom, expectations, education and physical environment. [see Richard Lewton's "Biology as Ideology-the Doctrine of DNA" 1991]. He argued that while traditional Darwinists portrayed the organism as passive recipient of environmental influences, a correct understanding should emphasise the organism as an active constructor of its environment. The organism –environmental relation is reciprocal and dialectical.

Cultural Determinism

The culture in which we are raised determines who we are at emotional and behavioural levels. We humans create our own situation through power of thought, socialisation and all forms of information circulation. Culture also influences social and political arrangements and religion, race, rationality, epics, customs and language determine national identity.

Chapter - 14

Human Development Paradigm

A paradigm is a new way of looking at a thing or issue; of asking questions appropriate to that framework. The term human development has acquired a significant popularity in today's contemporary world- a movement away from the earlier preoccupation with economic growth measured by Gross National Product (GNP) that was just the monetary value of all the goods and services produced within a country. Dissatisfaction arose with its inability to assess wellbeing of human beings beyond material goods and services. We may be producing weapons while there is mass hunger. Secondly, GNP does not focus on inequality or social justice. The expansion of an economy may be at the expense of sections of people. When there is extreme inequality, market economy (or for that matter even an authoritarian economy where a ruling class decides allocations of resources as in dictatorships) would use resources to promote the comfort and luxury and status consumption of the well to do who hold the strings of political and economic power. Market is not without the operation of power. Apart from national economies, even at global level income disparities are widespread. This requires a social safety net for poor nations and poor people. The ethic of development implies that industrially advanced nations design a more sustainable development for all.

Mahbub Haq along with Amartya Sen helped to shift the focus from growth to the non-material ingredients of what makes for real human development. One had to for this purpose, redefine the goals of development. Haq (2003) articulates the new thinking by incorporating Sen's notions of capabilities. In two influential publications, Amartya Sen elaborated his concept of capabilities and the functioning that enhanced those capabilities. Sen (1999) in his 'Development as Freedom' defines development as expanding people's freedom. This freedom is contingent on economic arrangements for education and healthcare as well as political and civil liberty. He sees development as a process of expanding the real freedoms that people enjoy. "In this approach expansion of freedom is viewed as both: (i) the primary end; (ii) the principle means of development.

They can be called respectively, the constitutive role and the instrumental role of development". (page 36)

People lacking opportunity to receive education that will open greater possibilities in their lives in terms of intellectual advancement as well as better work, are forced to be where they are, may be doing onerous ill paid jobs. Lacking income they cannot buy food or ensure better nutrition and when ill access healthcare. Economic deprivation brings un-freedom. Denial of political and civil liberties make it difficult for them to voice their concerns. Social values and prevailing mores determine the freedom people have and reason to value. Sen indicates five distinct types of instrumental freedoms–(1) political freedom (2) economic facilities (3) social opportunities (4) transparency guarantees and (5) protective security. These are instruments that advance capabilities and freedom. Freedoms enunciated above are not just ends but the very means of development. In making appropriate institutional arrangements, Sen emphasises that the instrumental roles of distinct types of freedom have to be considered, beyond the foundational importance of overall freedom of individuals. (pp. 37-40)

In another work, Dreze and Sen (2002) stressed the importance of people's participation in development as a critical issue because the basic problem of political marginalisation of underprivileged cannot be solved by marginalising them more by excluding them from political power. This implies that only through a participatory process can we expand the scope of democracy. Much will depend in India on to what extent it can push this process. Public participation has a crucial role to play in the multi-institutional format of development that incorporates markets as well as the government, media and popular organisations in the reach and effectiveness of each of these institutions and their joint functions. Economic development then must be seen according to Dreze and Sen, in terms of changes it makes to the actual opportunities and freedoms of people, according to class, gender, location, social status and other relevant distinctions. Freedoms are of different kinds and the distinct kind of freedoms help in enhancing and consolidating the freedom of another. These freedoms of different kinds are interrelated and mutually supportive. This interlinkage lies in human ability to make use of one kind of freedom to enhance others. In the following para, I cite Sen and Dreze's formulations and add my own examples to highlight their pronouncements.

The pernicious effect of inequality cannot be missed by any impartial assessment of social health. The Oxfam report on global inequality is a telling indictment of the state of affairs. While one in nine people do not get enough to eat, over a billion make do with less than $1.25 a day. The richest one per cent of adults in the world have been increasing their share of total wealth. In 2010, the richest 80 persons in the world had $1.3 trillion. By 2014, they increased their share by attaining a collective wealth of $1.9 trillion.The richest 80 persons have as much wealth as the total assets of 3.5 billion people. Pharmaceutical company owners in India head this list.

Data from credit Suisse show India's super rich, is richer than ever. The Bottom 10 per cent of India held 0.2 per cent of the country's total wealth in 2014 while the top 10 per cent held 74 per cent, the top 1 per cent held half of India's total wealth. (as reported in the Hindu November 8, 2014).

Inequalities affect freedom in three ways: (1) the distributional aspects of inequality. This is not only with respect to income but other physical or mental disabilities, (2) the unfreedoms of some in society contrasts with those who have, those freedoms like education for example. Extending freedoms widely across society involves eliminating the divisions between haves and have-nots. People with resources can afford to give their children expensive schooling. The others have to make do with poor quality schools, (3) Social change can come about only with social participation. Many regressive practices in India ended with such efforts by concerned citizens and

(4) Participation is connected to the demands of equality. Apart from basic level such as voting there has to be public action. One can appreciate the fact that the recent Right to Information Act has given the citizen a tool for such participation which Sen espoused. Political participation is more effective if there is some equity in economic resources. We are aware how those with clout can bend rules. It does not require great imagination to see how inequality in participation is aggravated by social divisions like caste, gender and other statuses like educational level and family background. Even though the ushering in of Panchayati Ṛaj (local self government) has given women elected representatives power, its exercise depends upon the actual force of patriarchy where men are reluctant to secede this power.

Development Dialogue had many critical essays on the model of development Dag H (June No. 47). To veer our concern away from growth the concept of human development has since been adopted by UNDP.

In the Human Development Report (2000) many of the ideas of Sen and Dreze find echoes. It begins by asserting human rights as basic to human development henceforth HD. They are compatible and congruent aspects of development. The idea of HD focused directly on the progress of human lives and well-being. Well-being includes living with substantial freedoms. Human development is also integrally connected with enhancing certain capabilities–the range of things a person can do and be in leading to a healthy life as Sen argued 'Capabilities include the basic freedoms of being able to meet bodily requirements, such as the ability to avoid starvation and undernourishment or to escape preventable mortality or enabling opportunities given by schooling.' (Sen 1999, p. 19)

Thus, the 2000 UNDP report, makes this two-way connection between capability and human development. In the ultimate analysis HD is concerned with all the capabilities that people have reason to value. One can cite an example here to support Sen. It is the greater freedom that women now enjoy at least among sections–that they can opt out of compulsory marriage or compulsory motherhood. Women now can exercise more agency regarding their own fertility, given education. This was unthinkable a few decades ago.

We can seek remedies only when we have accountability for failures in the social system from the different agencies which bear responsibility for actions and strategies. The report talks of how human rights amplify the process of development. Firstly, individual costs and returns and social costs and returns can be at variance. However, advocates of human rights will insist that the abrogation of an individual's rights on behalf of some social goal has limits. Just now, we see how corporate giants in India are taking agricultural land that farmers are reluctant to part with because the costs of surrendering land far outweighs the social goal of an industry to provide some industrial goods and some jobs. The government is supporting the Corporate groups in this action as against the interest of land holding farmers and food security for a largely agricultural population. This has provoked massive agitations in parts of the country. The new Land Bill seeks to dilute many protective clauses in earlier act by eliminating the need for social impact assessment when land is taken away for industry and inadequate compensation for landowners. India still has a 45 per cent of the population in agriculture which for want of adequate investment in suitable technology for improvement in soil health, minor irrigation, affordable inputs which would increase productivity and lessen migration to urban areas. Non-farm employment in rural areas not having been developed with markets for inputs and outputs and storage facilities, labour productivity has declined. Additionally, under neoliberal regime and opening of international trade, capital goods are cheaper and organised manufacturing sector has shed workers and have preferred capital intensive production. Much can be put on the debit side for an economy unable to provide employment or sustain the livelihoods of people. A higher 'growth' hides these faults in the system. In other words, development is not inclusive. Secondly, there is a distinction between how institutions and officials treat citizens and how they affect them. Human rights enforcement traditionally monitor the conduct of public officials and the institutional structure. While upholding human rights ensure the entitlements of individuals, their effectiveness depends on appropriate social conditions. The right of a female fetus or infant to live is considerably reduced given the social preference for a male child despite laws prohibiting such action.

The UNDP report (2000) lists the basic freedoms that will merge human rights and human development by arguing that human development depends on securing some basic freedoms such as:

(i) freedom from discrimination by gender, race, ethnicity, national origin or religion,

(ii) freedom from want –to enjoy a decent standard of living,

(iii) freedom to develop one's human potential,

(iv) freedom from fear of threats to personal security, from torture, arbitrary arrest and other violent acts,

(v) freedom from injustice and violation of the rule of law,

(vi) freedom of thought and speech and to participate in decision-making and from associations, and

(vii) freedom for decent work without exploitation.

'The mark of all civilisations is the respect they accord to human dignity and freedom'.

Long ago CEM Joad had a felicitous phrase in his 'Guide to Modern Thought' – treacle toffee civilisation' to refer to those societies that prided on their artifacts but denied human rights and genuine human development. (Joad, 1933) We may ask agreeing with him: what use are magnificent cathedrals if millions die from neglect, hunger and exploitation?

The Connection Between Growth and Human Development

Obviously wealth has to be created if human beings have to live and live a rewarding life. The questions are: how is it created, what does it include, who gets share of it and at what price. Economic growth is about wealth creation. More than any other system capitalism has been enormously effective in channeling the irrational drives of the human psyche into an agency of unparalleled excellence for advancing material betterment. Although the market mechanism has produced mammoth misdirection of effort, it has also performed prodigious social co-ordination. This general capability still seems useable for some time. Although acquisitiveness has been useful, it too has a threshold beyond which it cannot adapt to maintain order. There is a distance between the behaviour and attitudes that a capitalistic society requires and those it tolerates at its own peril.

These words were spoken by no less a person than Heilbroner (1993). The difference between life expectancy in rich and poor countries will paradoxically be easier to achieve than erase the difference within the same society, between upper and lower classes. This has been a century of the common people. Who are the common people? The symbol Eric Hobswam chooses as symbol of what is common across the globe is 'mother and children'. The people who have most in common are mothers, wherever they live on this earth. In part a mother's experience reflects what has happened to a large part of humanity. The inequality of opportunity is one of the crucial factors in the future of mankind (Hobswam, 1999). Picketty (2015), showed how inequality is a social and historical phenomenon embedded in the larger canvas of wealth flows and income distribution. Inequality inhibits human development for many while a few corner resources. In a market economy, those with money power can influence what goods will be produced. These would be luxury goods and not what the majority need. Several alternate models have been proposed. For example, Gandhi felt that village, based production and consumption and revival of crafts would create a better society.

The poor spend a sizeable part of their income on health expenditure. In fact, people can fall in and out of poverty because of the need to spend their own resources on health in the absence of adequate and quality public health services. (Krishna J., (2003).Where women control household income they spend more on children's education (Strauss and Thomas, 1995). Economic growth is only an instrument for achieving development. Households, government, NGOs and community organisations are all involved in contributing to human development through growth. Social protection is important to alleviate the painful process of economic transformation which is accompanied by replacement of one type of activities by another. Overtime, economic growth may create new jobs but there is an inevitable lag between the destruction of old jobs and the creation of new ones. In the economic history of Europe, industrialisation was accompanied by the decline of agriculture in terms of both employment and contribution to national income. Social protection alone cannot recreate livelihoods. Following this analysis, Dev Nathan (2014) stresses the importance of social protection for the displaced while at the same time efforts are made to facilitate people to move the low productivity sectors to higher productivity sectors. Social protection has to be broad based and not just for unorganised sector of the economy otherwise the barriers to formalisation will not be removed. Social protection is now household based and includes subsided food, kerosene, gas etc. Research has attributed the availability of mid-day meals for school children for improvement in educational attainment of children which helps to enhances the quality of the work force and public healthcare augments as well as labour productivity.

In the nineteen nineties, HDR suggested five pitfalls that developing countries should avoid: (1) jobless growth, (2) ruthless growth that exacerbates inequalities, (3) futureless growth that ignores environmental concerns, (4) voiceless growth where weaker sections do not get empowered, and (5) rootless growth that erodes values and cultural foundations of society.

There is a direct relation between the expenditure on human development and reduction in poverty. Poor households spend a disproportionately higher proportion of incomes on human development–for instance, on food and health. This is more true of women in the household who spend on food and education than on cigarettes, alcohol and other wasteful expenditure indulged in by many men. With high levels of poverty, the spending on human development tends to be low both at private and public level. The nature of the growth process determines how the growth is translated in the economy. Government allocation for human development is through public expenditure. There are three ratios that express this: (1) *The public expenditure ratio:* as proportion of GNP by different levels of the government, (2) *The human development allocation ratio:* proportion of total government expenditure going to human development sectors, (3) *The human development priority ratio:* proportion of total human development sectors going to priority sectors like education and health.

Many studies indicate that increase in incomes result in improved education that opens up possibilities for improvement in one's situation. A study in Columbia found that a health and nutrition programme increased the life time earnings of individuals from

2.5 to 8.9 times than those of an illiterate worker. In India, mid-day meals in schools have noticeably increased school attendance of children from poor families.

However, there is no automatic transfer from improved HD into growth. If we wish to rethink development we have to address the right to development for everyone and every nation. It implies unequivocally that development assumes a human dimension when it encompasses material well-being in all low income countries such as food, health, education or the duration and dignity of life. These are not inherent in development and will assume such a human dimension only when through vigorous human activity it seeks to establish for men and women the world over the conditions essential to maintenance and blossoming of life. Without eradication of extreme poverty this ideal will not be achieved. There has to be fair practices in international trade, assistance to share resources from those countries to those who need them. Social welfare treats people as beneficiaries. Attention only to basic needs neglects the other human aspects of freedom, capabilities and enlargement of choices. Labour in less developed countries receive low wages, hardly sufficient to promote human development. Wage earning employment is today more intense and more complex and demands involvement. Market economies see labour as only a resource for production for profit. Layoffs hurt workers if there is no social security. One cannot achieve human development if in the process of creating wealth human costs are intolerably high.

Chapter - 15

Limits to Development as We Know It

It is only recently that we have come to understand the ecological limitations. We cannot exploit natural resources beyond a limit for these require time to regenerate. We have to acknowledge as we pointed right in the beginning the unity of life in this world and our responsibility to safeguard our heritage. We are now confronted by the need for ethical dimension in development in the pursuit of growth, both human and physical resources in entire areas of the planet are destroyed. This unilinear approach causes bias especially towards new technology and modification of land. The amount of waste we have created by technological growth augurs ill for us. Nuclear waste, plastic waste, electronic waste all add to the earth's enormous burden of bio non-degradable waste. When we think of development we typically think about progress, growth and expansion and assume that it provides a better life. Development should mean coming into being to realise potentialities and bring into fuller more stable state (Hatcher, 2002). We are also aspiring for human emancipation. According to evolutionary biologists like Jared Diamond, humanity's saving grace is our ability to get feedback and act upon it (Diamond, 2005).

Kothari (2013) points to India's record in development by drawing up a balance sheet of positive and negative outcomes. In terms of forest cover, consumption of ozone depleting substances, access to safe drinking water and sanitation facilities some substantial progress has been achieved. However, CO_2 emissions continue to be worrisome. By 2020, it is targeted that some improvement will take place for 100 million slum dwellers based on the improvement that have taken place during 2002-08.We can add to Kothari's balance sheet, how India has 988 species on the Red List and more than 50 per cent increase in the number of threatened species. Kothari enunciates principles for ecological integrity as follows:

(i) Equity and justice to ensure equitable access of all human beings, in current and future generations for food, water, shelter, clothing, energy, healthy living, social and cultural relations.

(ii) Right to meaningful participation.

(iii) Responsibility of each citizen and community based on the twin principles of ecological integrity and socio-economic equity.

(iv) Respect for diversity of environments, ecologies, species, genes, knowledge systems, respecting both common custodianship and individual freedom.

(v) Collective and co-operative thinking.

(vi) Rights of nature to survive and thrive.

(vii) Resilience and adaptability.

(viii) Local, rural, urban communities, small enough for a face to face decision making.

(ix) Interconnectedness among various aspects of human civilisations- environmental, economic, social, cultural and political.

United Nations Development Programme (UNDP) promoted 'Human Development' approach right from 1992. It defined the focus of development as concerned with both developing human capabilities and with using them productively. Capabilities require investment in people so that people can contribute to HD. Today this approach is extensively used by everyone concerned with development, government and non-government organisation, media, development agencies and political parties, all over the world. It conceptualises development in a broad sense by widening the choices of people. It emphasises both on the formation and the use of human capabilities. The concept brings into focus the issues of deprivation and inequality, puts people, in particular the most deprived and marginalised at the centre of development intervention. It views progress not only in terms of fiscal deficits, GNP and inflation but also in terms of improvement in the lives of people, in their health, education etc. The approach brings people at the centre stage of development planning. The concept of Human Development draws on the magnificence of human potentiality amidst the widespread experience of narrowly circumscribed lives. Mahbub-ul-Haq has been the pioneering leader of the human development approach. Human development has been defined as widening the range of people's choices in all fields- economic, political, and cultural. It recognises that people are both the means and the end of economic development. Both developed and underdeveloped countries are concerned with human development. The ultimate purpose of human development is to treat men, women and children- present and future generations as ends to improve the human condition in order to enlarge people's choices.

Growth cannot be the sole agenda. Unfortunately, the concern of G-20 countries (who account for 85 per cent of the world's GDP) appear to be overly bothered by falling rate of growth to barely 2.5 per cent across the globe. The solution offered is to revive growth through macro policies (fiscal and monetary policies) and structural reforms which will improve total factor productivity, improve business environment, to stimulate private investment to add to public investment through pump priming demand. [World Bank blog "Let us talk development" (23/06/2015)]. The counterview presented the following in the same site by a commentator who expresses well my own view and of others who are disturbed by neoliberal ideologies which place emphasis on investment as the necessary spur to 'growth' and growth as a pre-eminent agenda. There is agreement among public intellectuals that what we face in India is weakness in governance and insufficient impact of civil society on critical issues. Growth implies asset creation and more consumption. After all human beings require only so much food, so much clothes, so much houses and so much transport facilities. Increasing production will inevitably mean processed food, refined products, more cars, more palatial houses and so on. But these will be only for the rich. While the anonymous commentator talks of the above dysfunctional growth, we also have to add the limits to growth due to our present population size and depletion of natural resources. The famous fable about King Midas, who was greedy and wanted a boon such that whatever he touched should become gold, soon realised his folly for his food turned to gold, all plants, animals were now gold and even his daughter turned to gold. In the oil rich Saudi Arabia, there was a report that the Sheiks had gold plated toilet seats. We need to pay more attention to better governance, environment, political economy that heeds the voices of dissent.

Despite the tremendous progress in various fields it is now being increasingly realised that economic growth does not trickle down and is not evenly distributed among all the sections of the society. Major sections of the society are not the equal partners in sharing the benefits of opportunities created by the process of development. The dominant pattern of development that only emphasised the increase in economic growth witnessed a challenge with the emergence of the human development approach. It is only in the past few decades that focus has been shifted by looking beyond economic growth. It was also realised that there is increase in the national incomes of many countries but at the same time there was no significant improvements in the lives of the peoples. It is now generally accepted that the ultimate purpose of development in any society is not only directed towards increasing the production of goods and services but also towards enhancing human welfare. It is now realised that there is a highly skewed pattern of distribution of income and wealth. The human development approach tries to concentrate also on the social and economic advantages of bringing about more equitable distribution. It also aims to enable the individual to realise his or her full potential. Individual is seen as a means as well as end of development. However, without education this goal cannot be achieved. Further good and quality education increases the opportunities for employment, including self-employment which also helps in developing and enhancing the skills of individual. If we apply the binominal distribution with regard to achievements in education, the well to do would harbour some low achievers and on the other hand the less well to do would throw up exceptionally bright children. One comes across newspaper reports of how a poor landless worker's child managed to do extremely well in his or her studies. The more widespread is educational opportunity the greater the chances for this to happen. Today there is talk of "knowledge society" where knowledge is at a premium where innovation becomes important to cope with rapid changes in society and economy. Without freedom to experiment, innovations cannot happen. There is an increased realisation that human welfare is the true end of development. Thus, in the present scenario emphasis is placed more on providing basic education, strengthening health services, sanitation and housing conditions to the most vulnerable sections of the society so that their status can be enhanced.

In its first ever report on human development United Nations Development Programme tried to raise an important question of how the economic growth failed to result in the required improvements in the human welfare. However, the human development approach is often criticised to be a sectoral development that is concerned only with investment in education, health, and other social services. In contradiction, human development needs to focuses on the creation of economic opportunities and ensuring participation of people in it. Thus, authentic human development encompasses all three aspects of development, namely economic growth, economic opportunities, and people's participation.

UNDP continues to add new dimensions to the concept of human development since its beginning of publication of human development report in 1991. New dimensions such as security and sustainability, gender empowerment and cultural liberties are added to the recent human development reports. Thus, it shows that human development is a dynamic and multidimensional concept. The rediscovery of human development is a tribute to the early leaders of political and economic thought. The idea that social arrangements must be judged by the extent to which they promote "human growth" dates at least to Aristotle (384-322 B.C). He argued that "wealth is evidently not the good we are seeking, for it is merely useful; and for the sake of something else".

Immanuel Kant (1724-1804) continued the practice of treating human beings as the real end of all activities when he observed: "So act as to treat humanity, whether in their own person or in that of any other in every case as an end withal, never as means only". In addition Adam Smith (1723-1790) propounded that economic development should enable a person to mix freely with others without being "ashamed to appear in public". Further such understanding also was reflected in the writings and economic thought of including Robert Malthus, Karl Marx and John Stuart Mill. The basic purpose of development is to enlarge people's choices. People choices can be valued in terms of greater access to knowledge, better nutrition and health services and security against crime and physical violence and political and cultural freedoms and a sense of participation in community activities. The objective of development is to create an enabling environment for the people to enjoy long, healthy and creative lives.

Income and Human Choices

The major difference between the economic growth and human development schools is that the first school focuses primarily on the expansion of only one choice i.e. income while the human development school focuses on the enlargement of all human choices i.e. economic, political, cultural or political. However, it is often argued that the expansion of income will automatically enable one to enlarge all the other choices as well. But this has not been the case for a number of reasons. Firstly, in any society the income is unevenly distributed. People with limited access to income will see that their choices are fairly restricted. Further it has been also observed that in many societies the economic growth does not trickle down. In addition the national priorities in terms of model of development adopted by the countries, also to a large extent determine why income expansion may fail to enlarge human options.

The human development paradigm performs an important service in questioning the presumed automatic link between expanding income and expanding human choices. Such a link depends on the quality and distribution of economic growth not only on the quantity of such growth. A link between growth and human lives has to be created consciously through deliberate public policy - such as public spending on social services and fiscal policy to redistribute the income and assets. This link may not exist in the automatic workings of the market place, which can further marginalise the poor. The human development paradigm questions the existing structures of power.

It challenges that economic growth is essential in poor countries for eliminating poverty or reducing the same. The quantity of economic growth is not only important but also the quality of the growth. It calls for pursuing various policies, which is needed to translate economic growth into people lives. Greater link between economic growth and human choices may require far reaching land reforms, progressive tax systems, credit and bank system which is poor friendly, removal of barriers (political, economic or social) which may restrict the poor from participation and increasing their access to opportunities etc. these are the fundamental policy packages, however there can be variation from one country to another. Firstly, people must be placed at the centre stage of development. Measures must be taken to enhance their people's participation in the whole process of development. The main focus of development policies must be oriented towards betterment of peoples' lives, not just expansion of production process. Secondly, human development is assumed to have two sides. One looks into the formation of human capabilities, such as improved health, knowledge and skills, while the other is the use people make of their acquired capabilities for their employment, productive activities. Thirdly, there is a need to maintain a careful distinction between ends and means. People are regarded as the ends. But means are not forgotten. The expansion of GNP also becomes an essential means for expanding many human options. But the character and distribution of economic growth are measured against the yardstick of enriching the lives of people. Fourthly, the human development paradigm includes all the aspects of society, i.e. social, political, economic and cultural factors. Fifthly, it is recognised that people are both the means and ends of development.

A Holistic Concept

The human development approach covers all aspects of development ranging from economic growth, international trade, budget deficits, fiscal policy, or savings and investments or basic social services for the poor. Economic growth only becomes one of the subset of human development. There is fairly broad agreement on the following some aspects of human development:

Development must put people at the centre of its concerns.

The purpose of development is to enlarge all human choices, not just income.

The human development paradigm is concerned with building human capabilities (through investment in people) and with using those human capabilities fully (through an enabling framework for growth and employment).

Human development has four essential pillars: equality, sustainability, productivity and empowerment. It regards economic growth as essential but emphasises the need to pay attention to its quality and distribution, analyses at length its link with human lives and questions its long-term sustainability.

The human development paradigm defines the ends of development and analyses sensible options for achieving them (Haq, 1995).

The human development paradigm consistently takes the view that growth is not the end of economic development. Proper management of economic growth is essential in order to fully exploit the opportunities for improved wellbeing. In many countries it has been found that there is no automatic link between economic growth and human progress. But few of the countries have been extremely successful in managing their economic growth to improve the human conditions. To create desirable link between economic growth and human development four important ways needs to be adopted.

In order to enable people to participate and to share the benefits of the growth process, it is necessary to emphasise on investing in education, health and skills of the people. China, Hong Kong, Japan, Malaysia have adapted this model. Secondly, efforts must also be directed towards more equitable distribution of income and assets, as it is also critical for creating a close link between economic growth and human development. In many countries such as Brazil, Nigeria, Pakistan where the distribution of income is uneven, higher GNP growth has failed to translate into improvement in peoples' lives.

Many countries with their impressive and significant social sector expenditure have managed to make tremendous improvements in human development. Cuba, Jamaica, Sri Lanka are some of the few such countries. An important way of improvement of people's lives is through the empowerment of women, which is one of the definite way to link growth and human development. If people can exercise their choices in the political, social and economic spheres there is a good prospect that growth will be strong, democratic, participatory and durable. In short, in the human development approach people are not analysed merely as the beneficiaries of economic growth but as the real agents of every change in society whether economic, political, social and cultural. It is fair to say that the human development paradigm is the most holistic development model that exists today. It is neither narrowly technocratic nor overly philosophical. It is a practical reflection of life itself. The Human Development Report published by the UNDP since 1990s have been the one of the most recent documents that elaborates on the concept of human development. (Haq, 2003).

Chapter - 16

Reflections on a New Agenda

The annual Human Development Reports have been a major force behind constituting one of the strongest voices that has advocated attention to the non-income dimensions of human well-being and raising dissatisfaction with the notion that human well-being is to be advanced primarily through expanding incomes.

The human development approach has been an application of the "capabilities approach" conceived by Amartya Sen. The concept of human development differs from the human capital, human resource development and basic needs approaches. Human development differs from other approaches in three important ways.

Definition of ends and means,

Concern with human freedoms and dignity

Concern with human agency –the role of people in development.

Human Ends and Economic Means: In the human development framework development is about peoples well-being and the expansion of their capabilities and functionings. Expansion of material output is treated as a means and not an end. The ends- means relationship is reversed in theories of human capital formation or the human resource development, which focuses on human beings as a means to economic growth. The human resource development approach emphasises how education and health enhances productivity, and have important value for promoting economic growth. The basic need approach focuses on access to social services to meet basic material needs for a decent life. However, it failed to explain why certain needs are important. On the contrary, the human development approach views investment in education and health as having intrinsic value for human lives (Sakiko and Shivkumar, 2003).

The human development reports have highlighted two central messages: defining well-being as the purpose of development and treating economic growth as a means. The most obvious policy implications of this ends-means framework is that economic growth alone will not be enough to promote human development. Greater attention needs to be paid to other human development goals. Focusing on human lives as the end of development can frame the analysis of almost any challenge and drive the agenda of policy concerns that will be addressed. Each annual human development report has carefully applied this framework to the chosen theme.

The HDR 1994 calls upon policy-makers and researchers to focus on the security of people. The HDR of 1995 marks a turning point because it brought in the link between individuals and development. The HDR 1998 focuses on the impact on people especially on the different burdens and needs of the under-consumers, who are not consuming enough even to meet basic needs and the over-consumers whose consumption is huge and growing. It has taken new approaches to consumption/environment debates which have been hitherto dominated by concerns about economic growth to expansion of consumption as sources of environmental stress.

The HDR of 1999 while drawing attention to the impact of trade and capital liberalisation on economic growth redirects attention to the changing opportunities in people's lives and raises concerns over new insecurities that are being treated. The 2001 HDR sees technology as a tool for promoting human development. It looks at public policies to "make new technologies work for human development". The report introduces a new measurement tool, the technology achievement index which focuses on how basic technologies are spread through a country. Human security is a major current of international deliberations, which have given rise to the establishment of two world commissions in 2000 and 2001.

Human Freedom and Dignity – including Social and Political Freedoms

Human development is motivated by the search for freedom, well being and the dignity of individuals in all societies, concerns that are absent from concepts of social development, human capital formation and basic needs. The human development approach also maintains that all capabilities expand human freedoms and emphasises attaining the full range of these capabilities, including social freedoms, which cannot be exercised without a guarantee of political and civil rights. From the beginning the human development reports have underscored political and social freedoms as integral to human development, recognising them as a policy priority.

Peoples Participation and Change

Intrinsic to the human development approach is the notion of human agency. People must be regarded as active agents of change. The concept of human development is concerned with human agency in diverse areas such as participation in the life of a community, in community decision-making and in collective action to promote change. Human being can be agents of change through both individual and collective activities through education and health that enhance productive potential, through knowledge that leads to betterment in health and through the use of civil and political liberties to promote political change. All the Human Development Reports have reflected on the issues related to individual and collective action. HDR 1991 focused on investing in education and health to ensure equitable access to all. It supports 20:20 initiative a major policy advocacy effort to raise expenditures on basic human priorities.

The Scope for Human Development

The HDR have emphasised capabilities related to education and health as well as the human centred approach to development challenges while paying much less attention to political freedoms, participation and the importance of collective action. The future agenda of HDR should be to give more balanced emphasis to political freedom and collective action. Over the next decade they can contribute more to development debates by providing innovative concepts, measures and policy analyses that focus on the instrumental value of these issues for development.

Refined Concepts and Definitions of Development

Modern international development began with a speech- the State of the Union address delivered to Congress in early 1949 by President Harry S Truman. The speech introduced a proposal called Point IV, which was about a new policy of helping "poor" countries, the "under developed" nations with foreign aid from richer countries. This patronising point of view of development or more rightly underdevelopment, ushered in a new perspective that all nations progress, just some more slowly than others and it is the duty of the faster, more developed to assist the underdeveloped. It also suggested that the worth of a nation is based on its production, its ability to produce something not whether its people are spiritually fit, its families resilient or its environment pristine.

Truman conceived of the world as an economic arena where nations compete for a better position on the GNP scale.

When we think of development we typically think about progress, growth and expansion and assume that it provides a better life for those affected by it. Applied in a corporate setting, development is seen as labour productivity, physical growth and profit. Of course, these viewpoints of development are not absolute and many believe that they are outdated to the point of being detrimental. Negative accounts of development come primarily from reports that it is synonymous with destruction of natural and cultural resources.

As human and physical resources are developed, entire areas of the planet are destroyed or drastically altered and cultures are disrupted. This unilinear approach to development thereby causes bias especially towards new technology and modification of land. Thus, a multidimensional approach to development provides us with an opportunity to view development in a broader perspective and includes politics, society, technology, environment and culture. The notion of development is synonymous with economic and technological growth where bigger is better and more is desirable. One of the major problems with regards to development is its conceptualisation and the way it is defined and how it is institutionalised by organisations and professions. Peet, regarded Development to be a grounding belief of the modern world and that progress has long since replaced God as the icon of our age (Peet, 1999). There is no more misused word in the English language than "development" whether one refers to development of land, humans or particular economy says Hatcher (2002).

Relook at Economic Growth and Development

For majority of the people development is often synonymous with economic growth. Many economists make a distinction between growth and development and on occasion their definitions appear to contradict one another. Growth is a quantitative measure that implies an increase in size by the assimilation and processing of material or resources. Development means to come into being to realise potentialities and bring into a fuller more stable state. According to Peet (1999), development differs from economic growth in that it pays attention to the conditions of production, for example, the environments affected by economic activity and to the social consequences, for example, income distribution and human welfare, human emancipation and finer ethical ideas and higher moral values. He opines that these self congratulatory views of development have been and continue to challenged, and increasingly becoming the subject of intense skepticism. These diverse definitions of development and growth are illustrative of their complexity and the uncertainty with which they have been used. Although the definitions appear disjointed it is clear that in most cases the idea of development is one of economics fuelled by corporate growth, productivity, efficiency and profit.

Chapter - 17

Social Institutions

Neoclassical economics ignored institutions. They are assumed away. However, we require answers to the following: How do alternate set of rules and economic organisations affect the allocation of resources; why does the form of economic organisation differ within the same legal framework? What is the logic behind fundamental social and political rules that govern production and exchange and how do these rules change? (Khan and Ansari, 2008)

We have discussed at length the concept of development, the components of Human Development, its scope, its ethical underpinning for equity and justice. For promotion of these laudable objectives, we need social arrangements that will facilitate people's participation. There has been some proponents of the theme of what is called 'social capital' to mean the aggregate of the actual and potential resources which are linked to the possession of a durable network of more or less institutionalised relationships of mutual acquaintance and recognition (Bourdieu, 1986). Before the modern professionalised courier system came to India, we had the 'angadias' who regularly sent money on the basis of such recognised friendly network. There are even today caste networks that act as mutual aid clubs. In Tirupur in Tamil Nadu, units producing garments have arrangements to share orders, this views social capital as resources accumulated primarily as a set of obligations from others according to the norm of reciprocity which agents can draw on to achieve their interests. There is strong objection to the use of the word 'capital' as an analogy for the following reasons: it does not have the primary characteristics of 'capital' as technically understood: (a) capital has a time dimension, (b) it requires deliberate sacrifice of the present for future benefits and (c) it is alienable in the sense that it can be transferred from one person to another. There appears to be no single entity called social capital but one can accept that there are such distinct notions like trust, norms, culture, community networks that compose non-market interactions in an economy. There are many perspectives that focus on different aspects of social interactions drawing from different analytical and policy implications.

It is difficult to get data on 'social capital'. Only surveys and economic experiments are possible sources but these tend to be experiential and subjective and economists are not particularly enthusiastic about the utility of such a concept. Probably, it may be useful to see these social networks as mutual aid societies.

Amartya Sen's formulations are highly abstract so how in fact would one operationalise them? What is significant about Sen's concept of HD is his emphasis on human rights and freedoms (Sakiko, 2002). The various HD reports pay special attention to basic capabilities–namely, to be knowledgeable, to live long and to have a decent standard of living. However, this exclusive focus on only three capabilities has drawn much flak. These measures were a sort of rough and ready indices and did not mean that HD contains only three capabilities.

To make HD a reality, the priorities of action must be the removal of restrictions affecting the lives of people. These restrictions are: illiteracy, ill health, lack of command over resources, social and political oppressions that restrict one's participation in the life of one's community and to exercise autonomy in making decisions about one's own life.

Two major criteria can be employed in deciding which capabilities are important: (i) capabilities must be universally valued by people across the world, (ii) the promotion of human rights. HDR emphasised the agency aspect. In changing policy, social commitment and norms we need collective action. The idea of agency here is about collective action. In today's context, many UN agreements reiterate the following:

(i) Priority to social development with the expansion of education and health opportunities.

(ii) Economic growth that generates resources for HD in its many dimensions. Political and social reforms for democratic governance. Equity in the above three elements with a concern for all individuals.

(iii) Over the years HD reports reflect changing circumstances–from public investment to incentives, from economic and social policies to political institutions.

As early as the late nineteen fifties, the Marxist scholar Raymond Williams placed weight on non-economic and subjective aspects of human activity as crucial for understanding production and reproduction of life. Instead of arguing that the material or economic base produces certain effects and ideology as part of superstructure, a cultural materialist would argue that ideology and discourses generated by social institutions are themselves located in material practices that have material effects that affect the economic structure of the base. (Williams, 1958). Institutions are vehicles for capability creation. If innovatively designed, local level institutions can play a critical role in expanding freedoms that will enlarge capabilities for livelihood generation as well as social security. Institutions are the formal or informal rules that guide how people within societies live, work and interact with each other. Informal rules are the behavioural norms accepted by society. Capabilities contribute to the functioning of individuals. The second arm of the triad is endowments or assets that an individual has. What brings these two arms together are the formal and informal institutions which promote or deter political freedom and economic facilities (Chopra and Duraiappa, 2008). We are not merely private individuals but participants in a shared national life as members, who have a collective will as well as individual stake in the decency and humanness of our policies and public arrangements.

There is a connection between individual and larger struggle. Debates within the classroom, family, workplace all have a crucial role to play in shaping the understanding of citizens who then carry that understanding into formal political activity. Our concern should extend beyond particular interest groups like women or marginalised sections but address a variety of policies that enable public participation, not only in the explicitly political domain and processes but on a wide variety of institutions. According to Zakaria, democracy is one public virtue to be distinguished from the other characteristics of political systems. (Zakaria, 2003) There is now greater tension between constitutional liberalism which stood for the rule of law, separation of powers, protection of basic liberties of speech, assembly, religion and property and the group interests contesting for power and share of privileges. All democracies are not liberal. What is lacking in our understanding is that the behaviour of human collectivities is driven by the power of self-interest and collective egoism. "As Neibuhr concludes whatever increase in social intelligence and moral goodwill are achieved in human history, they may serve to mitigate the brutalities of social conflict, but they cannot abolish the conflict itself. (Neibuhro, 1960). Democratic relations are still relations of power. Representative institutions do not necessarily promote a wide sense of inclusion in aspects of decision making. It is possible for the state to be coercively authoritarian despite maintaining the procedural aspects of democracy. Traditional political philosophy does not make room for incorporating social, economic and cultural aspects. (Shapiro, 2004).

Politics deals with issues like who constitutes the political community, what power relations exist within it, how collective interests are articulated, how opportunities and means are available for resolving conflicts and reaching group aims in a legitimate and effective manner. If we have to establish a modicum of global justice, poverty, environmental degradation and violation of human rights outside one's country cannot be dismissed as not one's concern. One's private actions are not immune from global consequence (Chella Rajan, 2007). Are we not facing this in the current crisis of climate change? In the unequal distribution of resources, in the existence of plenty in some regions, with hunger elsewhere, are we not violating the ethics in the use of earth's resources that belong to all? The consequences of connectedness which we call globalisation are today profoundly disturbing because they have taken the form of an enforced connectedness. Satish Deshpande had expressed the new globalisation we are confronted with this most ably. He depicted it as a kind of new regime, where the connectedness and linkages across different sectors, different communities, different questions, make themselves felt in hitherto unexpected ways and that the density and intensity of these contacts are at a level not experienced before. (Deshpande, 2008)

Contemporary efforts at poverty reduction unfold in a substantially globalised context of economy and society. Global relations affect poverty in many ways- through trade, direct investment and movement of finance capital. Global communications, global diseases, global migration and global ecological changes affect poverty reduction efforts.

There are international networks, non-governmental organisations, multilateral aid agencies and above all the UNDP's commitment towards the objectives of human development that make poverty reduction and human development a global issue. The international effort to deal with HIV-AIDS is one such example. Civil society can be conceived as a political arena of collective citizen action - it is the way people relate to governance apparatus in today's world. It follows that global civil society is an arena of political action that goes beyond the nation state. The Kyoto protocol on climate change is a good example.

What is necessary to deal with conflicts is the need for human groups –whether racial, national or economic- to develop a degree of reason and sympathy which would permit them to see and to understand the interests of others as vividly as they understand their own and a moral goodwill to affirm the rights of others. This does not imply foregoing one's own interests but to judge the claims of others from the perspective of the intelligence of the whole community. It is only when there is a growing rationality in our dealings with others that injustice can be wiped out. Procedures of electing a government through popular vote do not give the real substance of democracy. The Third Reich in Germany was democratic but unleashed Nazism and world wars and massacre of Jews. As society opens up, politicians scramble for power and use emotive issues to garner votes like appealing to group solidarity. This is the experience of Indian democracy. We began this essay emphasising that a moral order has to underpin human society. Modern democracies require that those with immense power in society embrace their responsibilities to lead, to set standards that are not just legal but moral. The solution lies in the kind of education, that would build an ethical base from which a universal ethic can appear, diffusing values that respect individual rights and the respect for human dignity.

Globalisation

Since the first industrial revolution waves of technological improvement have changed the boundaries of production and this has redefined the role of the state. Information technology has reduced time and distance. As Luo (2014) contends, while the information and communication technology has increased productivity, where billions of activities are linked with one click of the mouse, the obverse side is that this has increased the risks as much as it has increased opportunities of participating in the Global Value Chain (GVC) as previously sheltered market boundaries and geographic distances become less important. While it is true that the expansion of labour intensive production gave new employment opportunities for Asian countries, this did not result in social upgrading in terms of higher wages or social protection. In developing countries, this GVC did not translate into good jobs or stable employment. To add to what Luo has said above, I can add Indian experience of Special Economic Zones and the opportunities for exports did not improve labour conditions. This setting favours large, technologically advanced, professionally managed firms leaving the bulk of small producers to languish or come to grief. Workers can benefit from exports only if their working conditions in terms of wages, length of working day, work week and defined benefits obtain. To benefit from these new opportunities, the national governments would have to upgrade the skills of workers and provide necessary infrastructure.

Open society is based the recognition that we act on the basis of imperfect understanding. It is important for us to accept this imperfection and we constantly seek improvement with a willingness to submit to critical examination. UNDP's HDR (2001) proposed a Technology Achievement Index (TAI) to measure the progress made by countries in technological progress. The indicators used relate to technology creation as measured by the number of patents and royalties received per capita, extension and diffusion of old and new innovation and human skills in terms of mean years of schooling, enrollment in science, mathematics and engineering. India's rank is 63 TAI out of 72 countries. George Sores (2002) argues that our measures of technology creation should not be just patents, but relate to science for basic human needs, food, drinking water, shelter and work. We have to shift from the present one-sided emphasis on private science to public science where we pursue socially relevant technology and delivery systems. The threat from globalisation that we face is the question of quality and cost between products resulting from mass production technologies and those produced by the masses. For example, in India, 90 million tonnes of milk are produced by almost 90 million farmers of whom 90 per cent are women. In contrast, over 70 million tonnes of milk are produced in the US involving less than 200,000 persons. The total number of farm families in the US is about 900,000 in contrast to over 105 million in India. The agricultural commodities in India are the main source of livelihood for rural India. In this context, it is clear international trade agreements are grossly unfair to developing countries like India.

Whenever goods from rich countries flow without restriction to the poor countries, under trade relaxation, the poor countries cannot reciprocate by building their economies because of strong pressure from imports. Meanwhile, well to do countries that swear by free trade, are not averse to using subsidies that act as non-tariff barrier. Poor countries are at a disadvantage to begin with in gaining from exports that would relieve poverty and promote their economic growth. Globalisation has distorted the allocation of resources in favour of private goods and global financial markets are prone to crisis. Secret offshore bank accounts are used for a variety of illegitimate transfers deserve special scrutiny. There is greater need for countries to act collectively through international institutions but unfortunately this is the time when confidence in international monetary institutions like the IMF and World Bank is at its lowest.

Chapter - 18

Reality for the Common Man in India

A large majority of people in India suffer from abject poverty. Poverty has two dimensions–relative and absolute. According to 'The Human Development, Poverty and Unemployment' report by the Government of India (GoI, 2007) India had around 250 million people living in poverty, belonging to all faiths and region. According to the Government of India's committee set up in 2012, to look at methodology for assessing poverty, we have today 29.5 per cent of the people that exist below the poverty line defined as per capita consumption expenditure of ₹ 972 in rural areas and ₹ 1407 in urban areas at all India level. But according to UNDP which uses an enhanced matrix, the percentage of people who are poor in India is 55.30 per cent. This despite the fact that India in the past twenty years has risen to the status of a global economic power, shared with China. But there the comparison ends for China has achieved more in terms of Human Development than India. Let us look at the figures:

Table - 1

	India	*China*
Life expectancy	65.8	73.7
Maternal Mortality	21.2	3.7
Infant Mortality	42	13
Mortality of Children under 5 (maternal mortality is calculated per 100,000 live births)	43	4

Things have improved somewhat by 2010, maternal mortality was 167 per 1,00,000; infant mortality was 40 per 1000 live births.

Non-communicable diseases account for 60 per cent of deaths. Global evidence suggests that spending on healthcare by public bodies should be five to six per cent of GDP. In India, government spending is only 1.86 per cent of GDP, which is four per cent of total government expenditure (Thorpe, 2015).

India is far behind even Brics [Brazil, Russia, India, China, South Africa]

According to 2014 Human Development report of UNDP.

Table - 2

Country	*HD Index*	*Gender Development index*	*Per cent poor*
Sri Lanka	73	66	NA
Maldives	103	90	NA
India	135	132	55.30
Bhutan	136	NA	29.4
Bangladesh	142	107	49.50
Nepal	145	102	41.40
Pakistan	146	145	45.60

Human development index includes, life expectancy at birth, years of schooling, per capita income. The ranking is done for 187 countries. The top countries are in Scandinavia. When inequality is factored in, there is further loss in HD.

More recently a social progress index (SPI) has been compiled.

The criticism about human development index is that the weights assigned to individual components are subjective–if education is seen as important it will receive more Weight (Das, 2015).

The social progress index is a simple average of three components:

Basic Human Needs, Foundation of Well Being, Opportunity

Nutrition, medical care, Access to knowledge, information, personal rights

Air, water, sanitation, health, personal freedom

Shelter, eco-system choice

Personal safety, sustainability equity and inclusiveness.

As of now, India's rank among 187 countries on Human Development Index is 135! Twenty-nine per cent of our workforce (aged 15-59) are illiterate; 40 per cent have not gone beyond middle school; 90 per cent of our workforce is outside the coverage of any formal training. In other words, barring a section of a privileged class, a large number are denied equality of opportunity. Inequality has worsened over the years. The Richest 85 persons in the world own more than half of the world's wealth. In the richest country, namely the USA, in 2010, 93 per cent of additional income created went to the top 10 per cent. Inequality creates fissures in society, leaving those at the bottom feeling marginalised and disenfranchised. Joseph Stiglitz (Nobel Laurete) in his book, "The Price of Inequality" (2012) talks of how incentives are created for not creating new wealth but taking away from others.

He makes a powerful plea for paying attention to every one's self interest, in other words to the common welfare as a precondition for one's own ultimate well-being. It is not just good for the soul but it is good for business. He held Gross Domestic Product as not only an inappropriate measure but also an unsatisfactory measure of progress. He pleaded for infusing morality back into capitalism. He cites the example of Firestone Tyres company, which tried to reduce wages by 30 per cent as well as insisting on longer hours of work by workers. This resulted in defective tyres and led to more than 1000 deaths.

In India, adulteration in food is rampant to make quick profits. The adulterer of say cereals will face in turn, the adulteration of say cooking oil. Of all evils, making food hazardous for consumption is indeed the most heinous of crimes worse than murder. So often news reports in India tell us how many children were seriously afflicted by bad food, needing hospitalisation.

Inequality does not benefit even the rich- because extra incomes they get go to not satiate wants but to buy status goods- the latest car, the yacht, or what have you. What is not realised is when inequality is factored in, there is loss in human development. We cannot build our heaven on the misery of others. Buddhism repeatedly reiterated that our welfare depends on the welfare of all others. Human welfare depends on equipping our people with quality education, health and social protection from vulnerabilities of old age, illness, disability. Social protection at present in India is less than two per cent of our GDP, and covers barely four per cent of our population. Environmental degradation costs us six per cent of our annual GDP (Akhtar, 2014). Significantly, more inequality arises out of differences in opportunity rather than innate differences of talent or farsighted decisions of families. Only a small subset of influences on a person' income is beyond one's control. The unjustifiable part of inequality is linked to observable characteristics- inadequate access to means of improving one's chances in life; education, healthcare services, job opportunities, secure employment, availability of basic necessities like water and sanitation, housing, clothing, roads, transport and access to decision-making authorities. Most of these can occur only through collective decisions of society to allocate enough resources for those ends known as public goods. In addition to all these we need also an ethic of civic responsibility- an understanding that "I am my brother's keeper." We have to take care of each other and of the world we live in if humanity has to fulfill its destiny. We share this earth many others–living, non-living matter.

"Inequality is a social and historical, phenomenon and is shaped by the way economic, social and political actors view what is just and what is not as well as the relative power of the actors and the collective choices that result" (Picketty, 2014). The history of inequality says Picketty is shaped by the way economic, social and political actors view what is just and what is not, as well as who are the influential actors who make decisions.

Picketty's studies show that the rate of return on capital has been between four to five per cent while the growth rate was barely one to two per cent. Capitalism's destabilising force is precisely the unequal relationship between capital and labour. Capital reproduces itself faster than output increase. Income inequality is aggravated by the saving and investment patterns of the rich. This is because, the larger the size, the higher becomes the rate of return on investment. Higher growth does not result in social mobility as demonstrated by the experience of the USA. Inequality may be inevitable-for example, due to differences in native talent, but inequality of opportunities denies many a chance in life, to make the best of their own lives.

No doubt, outcomes depend on our own efforts and other people's efforts decisions.

In the recent years the creation and development of social infrastructure occupies an important role of planning. Efforts are now directed towards improvement in the social sector development focusing on the key areas of human development. There has been introduction of new schemes (such as the NREGS, NRHM) along with increased budgetary allocation, which aims at improving the life of majority of the population. In certain cases the coverage has been extended, it is made more accessible and such the delivery of services have also improved due to initiatives by civil society to undertake social audit.

India's 112th rank among the 152 countries in 2014 Global Human Development report shows the level of development of the country and its people. It has improved slightly since then. Further there has been the problem of widespread malnutrition and under-nutrition that also needs required attention and focus. Even today it has been shown by various studies that achieving universal elementary education is a distant dream. The schemes such as the National Rural Health Mission (NRHM) and Sarva Siksha Abhiyaan (SSA) aim to address these important problems. Further, the 61st NSSO survey also throws light on the jobless growth under reforms. The annual growth rate of employment is declining year after year. In addition, given this scenario of increasing unemployment there has been only marginal decline in the levels of poverty as well. According to our latest 61st NSSO survey 22 per cent of India's population lived below the poverty line in 2004-05. (GoI, 2006-2007). Further there has been the problem of widespread malnutrition and undernutrition that also requires attention and focus. Even today it has been shown by various studies that achieving universal elementary education is a distant dream.

From 1990s began the process of globalisation. India's record in human development has been unsatisfactory (see appendix). With the level of human development India has achieved so far, it has just managed to enter the categories of countries which are in the middle level of development but even this conceals wide variations across regions within the country. The growth performance and structural changes in the state domestic products of Indian states reveal the uneven development across states. With respect to social sector expenditure, there have been substantial changes in the composition of social sector expenditure. Not much increase is noted in our expenditure on health and education. More disquieting is the fact, that there has been underutilisation of resources. Absence of new schemes, absence of matching funds, lack of local infrastructure, lack of skills, lack of interest and delay in release of funds. As compared to 1980s social sector expenditure in 1990s has gone down (Pradhan, 2007). Even in 2000-2001, the total social sector expenditure remains less than six per cent GDP. While within this, education has the maximum allocation, to what extent delivery, utilisation and effectiveness are satisfactory, are moot questions.

Pradhan (2007) in his analysis of social sector expenditure in relation to human development in India brings out the unsatisfactory performance. If we take the record of the decade 1990-91 to 2000-01 the following facts emerge. Education (including sports) a major component of human development is barely 3.00 per cent of our GNP on an average; public health and water supply has remained around 1.15 per cent; family welfare claimed 0.16 per cent; social security and welfare hovers around 0.68 per cent to 0.76 per cent. Other social services did not by any means get pride of place with an average expenditure over the period 0.50 per cent. Basic minimum services got low attention with an average of less than 0.23 per cent. All in all on total social services our country spends 5.59 per cent of its GNP. Even these figures do not merit congratulating ourselves because between expenditure and the quality and outreach of services there is a chasm given inefficiency, corruption, poor infrastructure and so on. Over the years there has been a shift away from development. For example, within rural development outlay there is a shift from rural employment to housing, water and rural roads.

As for inequality the Lorenz ratio indicating concentration of income for rural India is 0.37 per cent and 0.39 for urban India. If we look at the distribution of households and income by occupation categories, self-employed farmers who constitute 30.59 per cent of total households in the country, receive just 36.11 per cent of the total income of the country. On the other hand, salaried households who constitute only 13.79 per cent of all households get 19.4 per cent of total income. Agricultural wage earning households who are 32.54 per cent of households, earn only 21.47 per cent income. Non-agricultural wage earning households who are 10.55 per cent of all households earn 21.47 per cent of income. (Pradhan and Roy, 2003)

Household income and its distribution is central to welfare analysis. It does not need any reiteration that self-employed farm income continues to be the major segment in rural India, but its level is inadequate to help in human development. The service sector now constitutes the major component of our economy in terms of income being 52 per cent of GDP. That without growth in manufacturing and in agriculture, India cannot meet the need for essential requirement of goods- food, raw materials and manufactured goods is clearly demonstrated by the share of income by income classes. The decline of agriculture in our national economy where agricultural self-employed farmers and agricultural labour who are the bulk of our population, receive income way below the salaried sector indicates a distorted distribution. (Pradhan and Roy, 2003). For the vast majority of South Asians agriculture is the main source of livelihood. There is strong evidence that in developing countries, which have achieved sustained growth, are generally those in which the rate of growth in agriculture exceeded population growth. These countries face demand constraints because international markets are flooded by agricultural exports from developed countries as we mentioned in an earlier section dealing with globalisation. There are five major considerations to be kept in mind for promoting human development according to Haq (2003).

High levels of human development cannot be achieved if development priorities do not focus on the occupation of the majority of the people farm or non-farm employment or where they live in rural areas. Policies on food security have focused on welfare approach and not empowerment of people by giving them the ability to buy food. South Asia has not enough cultivable land and is facing the negative consequences of chemical input based technology. Small farmers have to be the centre of revival for rural development. South Asia's trade and markets are not efficient due to internal and external causes. Despite critical importance of research and extension these are still woefully inadequate.

Lack of legal framework to define property rights and delay in land reforms has adversely affected the access of small farmers to employment. Strong economic growth is no doubt the prerequisite for human development in a country as it provides the required resources for improving the capability of people through education, health and social services. Education is linked to income earning capacity. The benefits of economic growth have to be equitably distributed through public policy initiatives to achieve maximum human well being. Obviously we have a long way to go. As we began saying, human development is not an individual effort–it requires the investment of resources material and non-material to improve the capabilities of all sections of society.

Chapter - 19

Gender Issues

Recent developments in policy literature have highlighted that poverty reduction and sustainable development should be the goal of governance. There are strong links between gender inequality and poverty reduction. General poverty reduction measures do not necessarily have an effect on female poverty. This requires strong political representation of women and governance structures and processes have to be made accountable to poor women. However, the effectiveness of women's participation in terms of their ability to articulate gender interests and the impact of this on actual resource allocation processes and decisions are critical. In the last few decades there has been an enormous research and data available on gender inequality in development. Women in poor countries are yet to achieve equal achievement in education, health and income. UNDP and national governments have regular gender development index to measure the disparity between men and women in various countries.

Understanding institutional rules, norms and practices in determining entitlements is the key to understanding gendered experiences and processes of poverty. Without a clear understanding of these institutional practices, merely targeting women is not helpful. Incorporating a gender perspective into governance cannot be restricted to any one domain but has to cut across all domains. In India, until recently women's issues were relegated to the Departments of Women and Child. We have to move from regarding the family as only a woman's domain. The recognition of gender bias in the family is the beginning point. Today intra household dynamics has attracted the attention of researchers but not yet sufficiently in policy.

Time- use studies in India have shown the enormous work burden of women in India especially rural women. A major problem which persist is the under counting of women's work in all our major national data systems. The blinkers that hide the reality of women's work are several: traditional notion of the male as the bread winner, much of women's work tends to be irregular and confined to the proximity of the household in rural India which gets clubbed as housework, enumerators' ignorance and women's own perceptions. In this context UNSNA (United Nations System of National Accounts) has helped by categorising women's labour into market work, extended market work and non-market work. It is the middle category where women fall through the net. Discrimination in employment, wages, opportunities for education and skill development disadvantage large sections of women hugely. Markets in fact act as bearers of gender. Civil society also reflects the social prejudices. Within the family, men are reluctant to share in the maintenance of household and child care. There is not enough effort to provide safe and secure environment for women, free from violence and abuse. Nutrition and rest for women of lower classes is a neglected area. Institutions and welfare arrangements fail to provide women effective options to quit unsatisfactory marriages. Patriarchal, patrilineal and caste structures produce gendered socialisation (Saraswathi, 1999)

Approaches to development and the methods that flow from them are shaped by assumptions that are made by people. Inclusionary and participatory approaches have a firm foundation in an assumption that human beings have capacities and value and potential and that for many, these are limited by being in a position of powerlessness, vulnerability or material poverty. These assumptions mean that conflicts of interest have to be recognised and addressed. All approaches to development have power embedded in them. (Rowlands, 1997). It is a question of what sort of power do they encompass, who is powerful, who is not and does that power help or hinder? People can change things if they can act collectively not only through formal political arena but all kinds of informal net work.

Chapter - 20

Future Agenda: Developing a Dynamic Perspective

Development is a 'whole' – it includes ecological, social, economic, institutional and political and this systemic inter-relationships and action must integrate those dimensions. Another development has these core principles:

1. Need orientation of human needs, material and non-material.
2. Endogenous- should stem from the heart of each society, its sovereignity, its values and vision of the future.
3. Self reliant: development of each society should primarily be on its own strength and resources.
4. Ecologically sound: resources of the biosphere must be utilised rationally in full of the potential of local eco-systems as well as global and local outer limits imposed on present and future generations.

Despite 189 countries signing the UNDP millennium goals development continues to be seen as linear. Markets no matter how fast they grow cannot distribute health, education, clean water, sanitation or shelter. In an unequal society with differences in income, wealth and political power, the market obeys he who pays more- or to him doth hath will be given principle. Need does not translate into purchasing power automatically. Market obeys demand backed by ability to pay. (Dag, 2006). Without policy intervention that redistributes resources, human development for many would not materialise. More and more saner counsels are being voiced even though they are unable to reverse the current paradigm of progressive commodification of natural environment and social relations. As Rist says, somewhere we have to begin to question the basic assumptions of mainstream economics. (Rist, 2006)

The core assumptions of mainstream economics as we have increasingly begun to realise are:

> Human beings live under scarcity and hence unable to satisfy their unlimited wants and hence economic growth is necessary. Scarcity is after all socially constructed. Advertisement, imitation, media all play a part in creating wants. Today we treat all exchanges as only money exchanges. This ignore other forms of exchange that have always existed in society like reciprocity, symbolic exchange, labour exchange and gift exchange in marital relations. In farming communities people work on each others' fields during harvests. I saw an unusual form of this among women. In a Gujarat village, women move from house to house helping each other to roll 'papads' – a savoury with pulses that can be fried or roasted and now exported). Is there some way by which services can be made to work for the poor?

Shantanarayana and Shah (2004) analyse why and how services fail in the first place to reach the poor. Governments do spend one-third of their budgets on health and education, which are accessed mostly by the poor but the richest fifth receives three times the curative healthcare subsidy of the poorest fifth. Even when public spending can be reallocated towards poor, money does not always reach the frontline service provider. If the share of public spending is increased, it does not guarantee that teachers and health professionals will do their jobs well because they are deeply mired in a system where incentives for effective service are poor and penalties for non-performance are absent. This is the case in India with government schools. In the city of Mumbai parents dissatisfied with government schools are increasingly seeking private schools and spending beyond their means to give education to their children. Municipal school buildings built at public expense lie empty or hired out to NGOs. The rare exception where people took the initiative to make public institutions work was in Kerala.

While the supply side has these defects on the demand side parents do not send children to schools for various reasons-expenses of books, travel distance of school and so on. The dropout of girls is more serious than that of boys because of low priority given to schooling for girls and girls' involvement in housework and sibling care. Recently mid-day meals to school children have been tried to improve school attendance of poor children. Some experiments have been made to improve the situation by transferring responsibility to lower tiers of government like the panchayat in India.

The definition of poverty embraces various aspects of the failure to pay the costs of a genuinely human life: hunger, sub-standard housing that keeps individuals and families in conditions of vulnerability, disease, greater or long-term disadvantage, inability to read or write, inadequate instruction or training, inability to participate freely in the life of the community because of the accumulation of handicaps. In metropolitan Mumbai 60 per cent of the people live in slums under sub-human conditions while high rise buildings keep arising all over. Yet it is these slum dwellers who provide all basic services to the well to do. Mismanaged planning of urban development, uneven regional development induces mass migration of people to seek their livelihoods where they can.

These states of affairs point to the failure of human rights for many. We have to appreciate that assessments of human development if combined with the human rights perspective can indicate the duties of others in society to enhance human development in one way or another. It concerns accountability, culpability and responsibility of those who have stood to benefit from development. Human rights approach implicates development in two ways:

> Individual rights express the limits on the losses that individual can permissibly allowed to bear, even in the promotion of noble social goals. Rights protect the individual and minorities from policies that benefit the community as a whole but places a huge burden on them. The number of people displaced cruelly due to development projects like dams, infrastructure like roads, or factories that take away agricultural land run into huge numbers. In many cases people affected are not even consulted or offered decent compensation. Rights distinguish between how institutions

Economic Growth Alone is not Enough to Reach Millennium Development Goals

Regions	*Annual Avg GDP Per Capita Growth 2000-2015 Per cent Per Year*	*People Living on Less than $1 a day*		*Primary Completion Rate*		*Under five Mortality Rate*	
		Target (per cent)	*2015 Growth Alone (per cent)*	*Target (per cent)*	*2015 Growth Alone (per cent)*	*Target (per 1000 births)*	*2015 Growth Alone (per cent)*
East Asia	5.4	14	4	100	100	19	26
Europe and Central Asia	3.6	1	1	100	100	15	26
Latin American and the Caribbean	1.8	8	8	100	95	17	30
Middle East and North Africa	1.4	1	1	100	96	25	41
South Asia	3.8	22	15	100	99	43	69
Africa	1.2	24	35	100	56	59	151

Note: Elasticity assumed between growth and poverty is –1.5; primary completion rate is 0.62; under five mortality rate is –0.48.

Sources: GDP Growth Projections from World Bank (2003) and Devarajan (2002).

and officials treat citizens and how they affect them. Human rights analysis can enrich our assessment of social progress. Human development is not always consonant with human rights. Just as human rights contribute something important to human development, the latter is important because it helps us to show how different policies affect different groups; it reveals the outcome of policy in human achievement of different sections. A balancing of different claims become necessary. While human rights are matters of individual entitlement, their fulfillment depends on appropriate social conditions. The goal of human development is to create an enabling environment. Human development has an abiding interest in progress.

Socialism as it was meant to be

Socialism is the view that the good life can be achieved here and now by collective and rational human action not for a few but for all. It is a substantive doctrine that undermines individualisms because they have no conceptions of collective human actions. At the same time it recognises autonomy and self-determination. What it is against is any concentration of economic and political power. Egalitarian principles are the hall mark of socialism as it is meant to be. Whatever was practiced as 'socialism' in countries violated these basic principles. The list of socialist values one can come up with are: life be free and democratic; there is value for individual creativity; individuals gain distinct identity; where people can manage their own lives both in the work place and outside; where work and leisure are not distinguished and finally organic links exist between self and others and human beings live in peace with nature. These are utopian views which no society can match. A good socialist society is imperfect because it projects the ideal of a creative human being. A socialist is supposed to sacrifice the imperfect present for a perfect future. These are heroic models. Representative democracy is the nearest we can come to for the values of liberalism that upholds individual interests. It is socialist reforms that will make capitalism 'bearable'. (Bhargava, 1992). Some still believe that we should reclaim the socialist vision (Michael, 2001). Two great features of twentieth century were: (a) the experiences of underdeveloped countries that strove for rapid industrialisation through a hierarchical model they labelled 'socialist', and (b) the failure of socialist democratic governments in the developed part of the world to do no more than tinker with capitalism. Karl Marx in his final version of the communist manifesto stated the socialist goal as "An association in which the free development of each is the condition for the free development of all". He believed in the development of human capacities as an end in itself. Increased productivity should not come at the expense of workers but should translate both into satisfaction of needs and also the possibility of freedom to be artistic, scientific and creative by the means created for all to aspire to these. "How better than to return to a conception of socialism where the full development of the human individual is paramount" (Michael, 2001).

Chapter - 21

Conclusion

This essay began by exploring the philosophical, psychological, biological and social science bases of human life. A long discussion on Buddhist philosophy brings to our notice the core principle of ethical living in our own tradition. The essence of that ethical basis of human life is the recognition of interdependence with not only each other but all, of creation. Nothing exists by itself. Secondly, Buddhist view draws attention to impermanence, everything changes. Our blood is changed every 48 hours; our cells die and are reborn constantly. Within the nucleus of the basic unit of life is emptiness. We construct reality according to our own perceptions which do not reflect reality. Our 'dependent origination' implies that everything is relative- nothing has intrinsic quality of existence. Our human brain has evolved through evolution but it gave us only an organ/body parts but our behaviour has to do with our adaptation to circumstances, and flexibility. Fitness is this adaptability according to biologists. The philosophy of biology notes the intricate co-ordination of our organs. Hitherto our actions, as though we owned this earth has brought in ecological crisis which has created a new awareness that our earth is a finite entity and we cannot plunder it forever. Human life and human development have significance only through an ethical under grid of wherein lies our realising our potential. One may call it spiritual basis. Material accumulation cannot take us towards this goal. Bhutan has set an example by replacing GDP with Gross Domestic Wellness as a concept. They have stopped destruction of forests; they follow a more spartan life to conserve resources.

India has a long line of sages who have bequeathed to us their wisdom. It is not necessary that we have to escape to caves or forests to meditate or wear yellow robes. Most of all what we need is the understanding that earth is home to many beings, many living, non-living things whose welfare is not only important for their wellbeing but also for us. Many different explorations that human beings have made through science reiterate the wisdom of our ancient sages. Wars, conflicts for power, pelf have brought untold suffering to millions. These inflict not only wounds on the 'enemy' but equally on one self. Consciousness is that ephemeral quality in us that defies definition but its recognition links us to this universe as the only one we know, this earth as the only home we have and we can nurse that reverence for this mystery of why we are here. "Bhoomi Mata Putroham Pritviyaah" (Earth is my Mother and I am the child of the Earth. Oh. Mother Earth May I tread lightly on you). Rig Veda Samhita, Vol. I.

Leonardo Boff (2008) has written beautifully about our relatedness to everything else, and about the necessity of an ethic of "care".

He finds the present attitude of neglect for the fate of those excluded from the benefits of economic growth as shameful and that this neglect arises from a disregard of public morality. Public life is governed by corporate interests and society is beleaguered by corruption and struggle between power groups. What is sustainable for society or the planet that produces for itself and for beings in the eco-system would be that we take from nature only what it can replace and show a sense of solidarity between generations since it preserves for the future the resources they will need.

Boff maintains that as everything that is alive needs to be fed, in the same way care, the essence of the human being also needs to be continuously fed. Care lives off maternal care, tenderness, caress, compassion, conviviality ad the right measure of these in everything. Without care, the human being wastes away and dies. There is a song in Tamil which says 'unless the mother cares, can the infant live?' There is no point in searching for the healing path outside the human being. The ethos is within us and we as human beings need to turn to ourselves to rediscover our essence which is found only in care.

Human development cannot be just 'me and mine'. We need collective effort to carry all of us forward. Appropriate policy that makes the state deliver social services, wide ranging participation of all sections of society in the critical decisions that are made on behalf of common goals, respect for human rights and a perspective on development that moves away from singular concentration on economic growth are some of the prime requisites. Human development is multidimensional- it is about who we are, what we can do, what is our potential, our relationship to the rest of the world- it is our connection to "jal, jangal, zameen, janwar and jan" [forest, land, animals and people] as Govindacharya put it in connection with the ongoing protest against development projects on the river Bhagirathi. The dam and power project mooted by Uttarakhand government will spell disaster as it will block the free flow of the river Bhagirathi from Gangotri to Uttarkashi. Human development is unviable, unsustainable unless we care for our source of life and all our fellow beings. It is about eradicating poverty and vulnerability for the majority, so their capabilities might flourish. India does not win anything significant in the Olympics because we bank on a few performing individuals instead of nurturing talent in every school, every child. Human development is about letting hundred flowers bloom. This wisdom has been echoed by many thinking individuals and by august institutions like the Human Rights Commission of the United Nations in 1986 which reiterated that development is a comprehensive economic, social and cultural and political process which aims at the constant improvement of the wellbeing of the entire population and of all individuals on the basis of their active, free and meaningful participation in development and in their fair distribution of benefits resulting there from.

We began with the questions that plague us: who are we, what are we, why are we here. The various answers given by different disciplines provide guidelines in how 'We Can Be" to fit better into this world we inhabit. Each age has to find answers afresh to the problems posed, partly by forces beyond our reckoning and mostly by our ignorance of nature's ways and our efforts to control nature. Despite different answers available to us, this essay regards them as skeins of varied hues and strength that can be wound together to form a coherent strand. What is that strand? It is a deep intuition that there is a unity in the scheme of things and we belong to a magnificent enterprise-by whom, we do not know. Why should that matter? Our job is to safeguard our lives here and now by living in peace and harmony with each other and with what exists. The earth is our only home and it is in our interest to protect it. We do not know whether the universe harbours other intelligent life. Does it matter? There is so much we can do to better life for many of us right here.

Appendix

The Human Development Index - goes beyond income as the only measure of development. Each year since 1990 the Human Development Report has published the human development index (HDI) which looks beyond GDP to a broader definition of well-being. The HDI provides a composite measure of three dimensions of human development: living a long and healthy life (measured by life expectancy), being educated (measured by adult literacy and enrollment at the primary, secondary and tertiary level) and having a decent standard of living (measured by purchasing power parity, PPP, income). The index is not in any sense a comprehensive measure of human development. It does not, for example, include important indicators such as gender or income inequality and more difficult to measure indicators like respect for human rights and political freedoms. What it does provide is a broadened prism for viewing human progress and the complex relationship between income and well-being. The HDI for India is 0.619, which gives the country a rank of 128th out of 177 countries with data (Table 1). Now in 2014, our rank is 112 out of 152 countries.

References

Akhtar, Shamshad (2014): Under Secretary, ESCAP's. Report in the Hindu, August 7.

Barnes Cary F (1965) : The Book of Changes I Ching. English Translation. New York, E.P. Dutton.

Bhargava, Rajeev (1992): Relevance of Socialism. *Economic and Political Weekly*, Vol. 27. No. 40, Oct. 3, pp. 2161-2163; 2166-2169.

Bender, F.L. (2003): The Culture of Extinction Towards a Philosophy of Deep Ecology. Amherst. New York.

Beufort, de Elaine with Arora Sofia (1996) : The Three faces of the Mind: Developing Your Mental, Emotional and Behavioural Intelligence. Quest Books. The Theosophical Pub. House. Wheaton, IL.USA.

Boff, Leonardo (2008): Essential Care. An Ethics of Human Nature. Waylor University Press, Texas, USA.

Chandavarkar, Anand (2007): Economics and Philosophy Interface and Agenda. *Economic and Political Weekly*, Vol. 42, No. 3, January 20.

Chellarajan Sudhir (2007) : Global Politics and Institutions. A Utopistic View. October 13, *Economic and Political Weekly*, October 13, Vol. 42, No. 41.

Chitkara, M.G. (2002): 'Suffering and Transitoriness of Life'- Encyclopaedia of Buddhism- A World Faith. Vol. xi, pp.173-174. New Delhi: A.P.H. Publishing Corporation.

Chitkara, M.G. (2003): 'Buddhism a Requiem for human relationship'- Encyclopaedia of Buddhism; A World Faith. Vol. xv. p. 154. New Delhi: A.P.H. Publishing Corporation.

Chopra Kanchan and Anant Kumar Duraiappa (2008): Operationalising Capabilities in a Segmented Society. The Role of Institutions. In F. Cumin, M. Quizubash and Sabina Alkire ed. 'Capabilities, Concepts, Measures and Applications.' Cambridge University Press, Cambridge.

Cooley, Charles, Horton (2009): Human Nature and the Social Order New Brunswick. (USA) and London Transaction Publishers. (7th Reprint).

Dag, H, (2006): What Now. Development Dialogue, June, No. 47.

Das, Maitreyi Borcha (2014): World Bank Blog. Let Us Talk Development, 18 December.

Davies, Paul (1987): The Creative Cosmos. New Scientist, December 17.

Deshpande, Satish (2008): Another way of Understanding Globalisation. In "Towards Engaged Social Sciences' National Institute of Advanced Studies. Report R1-08.

Dhammapada (1998): Thanissaro Bhikku. Barre. Dhamma Dana Publication.

Diamond, Jared (2005): Collapse. Viking, Penguin, New York.

Donahue, James (2003): Ethics- An Antidote to Scandal. San Francisco Chronicle, Thursday, December 25.

Deval, W. and G. Sessions (1985): Deep Ecology. Living As If Nature Mattered. Salt Lake City, Gibbs M Smith Inc.

Drengson, Alan (1995): The Deep Ecology Movement.

Frisk, Milton (2008): The Personal and Social in Ethics. Noted from Lecture, Department of Philosophy, January 17.

Gaarder, Josten (2000): Maya. Phoenix House. Great Britain.

Gadgil, Madhav and Ramchandra Guha (1995): Ecology and Equity. The Use and Abuse of Nature in Contemporary India.

Gilbert, Rist (2006): Prerequisites for Alternatives. Development Dialogue. June No. 47.

Hack, Susan (1998): Manifesto of a Passionate Moderate. Chicago University Press, Chicago.

Hanh, Thich Nhat (1998): The Heart of Buddha's Teaching. Broadway Books. New York.

Hatcher, Tim (2002): Ethics and HRD. A New Approach Leading to Responsible Organisations. Basic Books. New York.

Haq, Mahbub (2003): Human Development Paradigm. In Par Fukuda Saikiko and Shiv Kumar ed. "Readings in Human Development-Concepts, Measures and Policies for a Development Paradigm," Oxford University Press. Human Development Reports Office. UNDP, New York.

Heilbroner, Robert (1993): Twentieth Century Capitalism, Affiliated East West Press Private Ltd. New Delhi.

Hobswam, Eric (1999): The New Century. Abacus, London.

Huberman, Leo (1936): Man's Worldly Goods. Harper and Brothers New York.

Human Development Reports. Abstracts 1999-2007: Web site, http// hdr.undp.org.en

Iliah, Kanchan (2001): God as Political Philosopher. Samya, Kolkata.

Jatava, D.R. (1998): 'View of the Universe.'- "The Humanism of Buddha", p. 28. Shree Publishers, Jaipur, India.

Jatava, D.R. 1998: 'Pyramid of Values.'- " The Humanism of Buddha." pp. 64-65, 69-70. Jaipur, India: In Shree Publishers.

Joad, C.E.M. (1933): Guide to Modern Thought. Fredrick A Stokes and Co. New York.

Judson, Olivia (2009): "Microbes and Me" Sunday Express, July 26, p. 13. [Reproduced from New York Times].

Kalpakam, Sankarnarayan and Parineeta Deshpande (2007): Pratityasamutpada – Dependent Origination.(ed), Somaiya Publications. Pvt. Ltd. Mumbai.

Katz, E, Alight et al (2000): Beneath the Surface. Critical Essays on the Philosophy of Deep Ecology. Cambridge, Mass, MIT.

Keown, Damien (2005): Buddhist Ethics. 6A very Short Introduction. Oxford University Press. Oxford.

Kolakowski, Leoszek (2009): A biographical note by Pratap Bhanu Mehta. *Indian Express*. July 21, p. 11.

Kothari, Ashish (2013): Development and ecological sustainability in India. Possibilities for post 2015 framework. *Economic and Political Weekly*, XLVII, No. 3, July 27, pp. 144-154.

Krishna, Anirudh (2003): Falling into Poverty. *Economic and Political Weekly*, Vol. 38, No. 6, Feb. 8.

Lewton, Richard (1991): Biology as Ideology. The Doctrine of DNA. Concord Publishers. Ontario.

Luo, Xubei (2014): World Bank Blog. Let us talk Development. 20 May.

Levine, David (2002): Economics and Game Theory. Open Book Publisher. UK.

Michael, I. (2001): Reclaiming a Socialist Vision, Monthly Review, June.

Nagarajan, Aravindan, Kaml K Kumara, T. Jayaraman, Goutham Radhakrishnan. (2015) "Appraising the Debate on Biodiversity, Conservation in the Wesetrn Ghats" *Economic and Political Weekly*, Vol. 50. No. 30. July 25.

Nathan, Dev (2014): "Social Protection for Economic Transformation." *Economic and Political Weekly.* Vol. 49, No. 38, pp. 19-21.

Neibuhr, Reinhold (1960): Moral Man and Immoral Society. Charles Scribner and Sons. New York.

Naess, Arne (1989): Ecology, Community and Life Style. Outline of an Ecosophy. Translated by D. Rothenberg. Cambridge, Cambridge University Press.

Nelson, C. (2006): Eco Feminism vs Deep Ecology. Dialogue. San Antonio, TX. St. Mary's University, Department of Philosophy.

Nohia and Lawrence (2001): Driven. How Human Nature Organises Human Behaviour. [Quoted in "From Servants to Masters. The Evolution of Professional Management in India." Global Business Press. All India Management Association, 2007]

Omvedt, Gail (2003): Buddhism in India. Sage, New Delhi.

Oxfam (2015): Reported in the Hindu, January 20. [presentation on the eve of the Global Economic forum]

Pani, Narendra (2006): On Intuition in Development Economics. *Economic and Political Weekly*, April 15, Vol. 49, 15.

Panmore, J. (1974): Man's Responsibility for Nature. London, Deeckworth.

Peet, Hartwick (1999): Theories of Development. Guilford Press, New York.

Popper, Karl (1945): Open Society and its Enemies. Princeton University, Princeton.

Pradhan, Rudra Prakash (2003): India's Human Development and Social Development Expenditure. *Man and Development*. Vol. 39. No. 1.

Pradhan, Vasant K. and P. K. Roy (2003) : Household Income and Its distribution. MIMA India. Survey Report. NCAER. Tata McGraw Hill Publication. New Delhi.

Pratap Singh, Uday and Sumar Singh (2015): Human Ecology and Development in India. (accessed from books.google.co.in)

Robinson, Joan (1962) : Economic Philosophy. Double Day and Co. U.K.

Rowlands, Jo (1997): Beyond the Comfort Zone. In 'Development Methods and Approaches.' Reprint. Rawat Publication.

Saikiko, Fukuda Parr and Shiv Kumar (2003): Rescuing Human Development from Human Development Index. Reflections on a New Agenda. In 'Readings in Human Development. Human Development Office, UNDP Office. New York.

Sange, Peter, C.Otto Schermer, Joseph Jawarorski and Betty Sue Flowers Presence (2004): Double Day. New York.

Saraswathi, T.S. (1999) ed.: Culture, Socialisation and Human Development. Theory, Research and Application. Sage, New Delhi.

Satyanarayanan, D. and Shekar Shah (2004): Making Services Work for India's Poor. *Economic and Poliitcal Weekly*, Vol. 39, No. 9. February 28–March 5.

Segan, Carl (1990): Pale Blue Dot. Uploaded You Tube July 19, 2011.

Sessions, G. (1995) ed.: Deep Ecology for the twenty first Century. Deep Ecology for the 21st century. Gibbs. Salt Lake City.

Sen, Amartya (1999): Development as Freedom. Alfred A. Knof. New York.

Sen, Amartya and Jean Dreze (2002): India Development and Participation. Oxford University Press. New Delhi.

Shapiro, Ian (2004) : Definition of Enlightenment. In 'Moral Foundation of Politics'. Aakar Books, Delhi.

Sheldrake, Rupert (1988): "The presence of past: morphic resonance and the habits of nature," New York Times Book.

Stiglitz, Joseph (2012): The Price of Inequality. New York. W.W. Norton and Co.

Singer, Peter, C. Otto Scharma, Joseph Jawarski and Betty Sue Flowere; Sogyal, Rinpoche (1988) : The Tibetan Book of Living and Dying. Rider. London.

Somaiya, S.K. (2007) Presidential Address. - 'Pratityasamutpada-Dependent Origination' p. x/v.

Sores, George (2002): On Globalisation. Review by Joseph Stiglitz. New York Times Review, May 23.

Strausss, J. and D. Thomas (1995): Health, Nutrition and Economic Development. RAND, Labour and Population Programme Rangarajan, Mahesh ed. (2006): Battle Over Nature, Sciencc and the Politics of Conservation. A Reader, Permanent Black, New Delhi, Rangarajan Mahesh, N. Balakrishnan, Deepa Bhatnagar ed. (2012): Environment History of India, Vols. I and II.

Tarthang, Tulku (1991): Skillful Means. Patterns for Success. Dharma Publishing. Berkeley, California 94704, USA.

Taylor, B and Zimmerman, M (2005) ed.: Encyclopaedia of Religion and Nature, Vol. I, pp. 456-60, London, Continuum International.

Upadhyaya, Kavitap: "Environment Ministry pushes for Contentions Hydel projects." *The Hindu,* Monday Aug. 10, 2015, p. 9.

Williams, Raymond (1958): Culture and Society. Chatto and Windus, London.

Wilson, Edward (2003): The Future of Life. Abacus. Times Warner Group. U.K. edition. New York.

Wilson, Edward (2004): On Human Nature. Harvard University Press, Cambridge Mass. and London. (originally published in 1978. Reissued with a new preface).

Wright, Robert (1994): Why we are the way we are. The New Science of Evolutionary Psychology. Vintage Books. A Division of Random House. Inc. New York.

Ye-sher Gyal-mtshan (1975): The Necklace of Clear Understanding. Translated by Herbert V. Gunther and Leslie S. Kawamura.

Zakaria, Fared (2003): The Future of Freedom. Illiberal Democracy at Home and Abroad. Viking/Penguin India. Amherst. New York.

Index

G

H

N

O

P

T